Movements of the Gospel

EXPERIMENTS IN MINISTRY
IN UNFAMILIAR PLACES

EDITED BY STEPHAN PUES
AND BRANDON J. O'BRIEN

Copyright © 2019 by City to City Europe
Published 2019 by
Redeemer City to City
1166 Avenue of the Americas, 16th Floor
New York, NY 10036

All rights reserved. No part of this publication may be reproduced, distributed, or transmitted in any form or by any means, including photocopying, recording, or other electronic or mechanical methods, without the prior written permission of the publisher, except in the case of brief quotations embodied in critical reviews and certain other noncommercial uses permitted by copyright law.

Print ISBN: 9780578539782
Ebook ISBN: 9780578539751

Contents

*   **Introduction: Europe as the Missional Frontier**
     Timothy Keller   8

1. **How the Gospel Makes Us More Creative**
   Stephan Pues   16

2. **At the Intersection of Faith and Culture: A Vision for Christian Cultural Expressiveness**
   René Breuel   36

3. **Integral Life: Building Multi-Ethnic Christian Communities**
   Jurjen ten Brinke   52

4. **Developing Gospel-Shaped Social Businesses in the City**
   Seán Mullan   70

5. **Transforming the Gap: The Arts as Mediator between the Church and the City**
   Sude Hope   96

*   **Notes**   120

*   **Bibliographies**   124

*   **About the Authors**   131

This collection of essays was created for the City to City Europe conference in Krakow, Poland from 30 October to 1 November, 2018.

It represents the perspectives of church planters and practitioners pioneering new kinds of ministry throughout Europe in the early twenty-first century.

Introduction

Europe as the Missional Frontier

TIMOTHY KELLER

Western culture poses a unique challenge to Christian mission. All previous cultures have shared some belief in a transcendent dimension to reality and have agreed that the individual should submit his or her personal interests and desires to the moral norms of that "sacred order." J. H. Bavinck spoke of "magnetic points," a kind of religious consciousness, that most people seem to share: a common belief that there is a supreme power or God; that there are moral norms to which we are beholden, and therefore a need for redemption; that we are part of a greater spiritual whole.[1] That means even when working in cultures dominated by other religions, Christians could still assume that people shared some general beliefs in God and moral truth, in sin and guilt or shame, and in an afterlife.

That is not the case in late modern or postmodern Western culture. Western culture not only denies the transcendent dimension, but sees the very idea of external moral norms and absolutes as an oppressive force from which to be liberated. In short, every previous culture had some idea of salvation from sin, while secularism says we need to be saved from the idea that we need salvation. And, of all religions, Western culture is formed in opposition to Christianity in particular.

In the late-modern West, we meet for the first time a culture that is not pre-Christian but post-Christian. Because Western society has tried Christianity and found it wanting, its people are especially impervious to it. To them, God is irrelevant. Religion is no longer considered something with social benefit but rather the very opposite. When Christians talk to Hindus, Muslims, or Buddhists, everyone agrees that they have different faiths. Secular beliefs, however, are not visible to Western people *as* beliefs. Their commitments regarding human reason, human nature, individual rights, and a materialistic universe are considered givens, "the way things are," and common-sense truths that require no faith. The religious consciousness that Bavinck saw in non-Christian cultures in the past seems to be receding in the West.[2]

While Western culture includes North America and Australia and exists in other pockets, it is in Europe that we see what we might call its most advanced social forms. There the church has struggled the most to transition from being chaplains of officially Christian cultures to being missionary communities. No one knows if North America and the great global cities of Asia, Latin America, and Africa will become as secular as Europe, but it feels to me as if Europe is the missional frontier for the whole Christian church. We must watch the European church and learn from its successes and failures because our own cultures are shaped by the same secularism and materialism more and more. This volume is an enormous help, then, for those called to do gospel ministry both inside and outside of Europe.

As an American, I most appreciate the lack of triumphalism in these chapters. Pride goeth before a fall, and in parts of the world where churches can and often grow large, it is common for Christians to talk arrogantly about the universal relevance of their particular ministry model and how worldwide revival is almost within our grasp. Our brothers and sisters in Europe can teach us a rightful humility.

But I also appreciate the absence of defeatism here. European churches can often fall into this discouraging error—cultivating low expectations and having a bleak outlook. That attitude is happily missing in this volume. Instead, you have stories filled with hope, even if the early successes chronicled here are still modest.

This non-triumphalistic hope is called for by 1 Peter 2:11-12:

> *Dear friends, I urge you as foreigners and exiles, to abstain from sinful desires, which wage war against your soul. Live such good lives among the pagans that, though they accuse you of doing wrong, they may see your good deeds and glorify God on the day he visits us. (NIV)*

The early church was neither a wholly despised nor a wholly attractive community. It was both. It was highly offensive and compelling at the same time. It was vilified and influential. Its sexual ethics, for example, were seen as cold and severe, yet the deeper moral logic behind them—equality, freedom, and love—was attractive, too. The very terms "foreigners and exiles" in verse 11 convey this dynamic tension because it means resident aliens—neither travelers without roots nor full natives.

Today, in the face of the great challenges posed to us by late modern Western culture, there is much debate about what the church's missional stance should be. Voices at one end of the spectrum argue that many of the ancient positions of Christianity—on sex and morality, on belief in the authority of Scripture, on the literal resurrection of Jesus, and on salvation through Christ only—must be abandoned or the church will atrophy and die. At the other end of the spectrum are those who see any effort to influence society or any expectation of significant church growth in our current culture as hopeless and hopelessly compromised. Neither approach thinks it will be possible to see what the early church saw—both persecution and traction, exclusion and growth.

The European leaders writing in this volume have avoided both of these wrong paths. In some ways, the change in European culture has helped them. The dynamic in 1 Peter 2:11-12 would not be as evident in an extremely hostile environment where there is no religious freedom at all (such as under ISIS), nor in a culture where the king has decreed that all institutions and leaders must be Christian. European cultures fall somewhere between these extremes today.

We should all aim, then, to see this dynamic at work. We should reject the triumphalistic calls (usually raised in the U.S.) to "take back the culture," as if that were possible or desirable. But we must also resist the temptation to withdraw from public engagement and expect little evangelistic fruit. Again, as an American, I believe I can learn a great deal from my European friends and leaders who are applying 1 Peter 2:11-12 and showing us all a way forward.

Chapter 1

How the Gospel Makes Us More Creative

STEPHAN PUES

Why Creativity Is Important

Creativity is hip. A lot of people talk and think about it. Innovation hubs for entrepreneurs launch startups and test creative ways of leading meetings and developing processes. Every young leader is educated in creative thinking. Creativity is no longer just a thing that painters, musicians, or writers use. It seems to be important for everybody.

Richard Florida, in his book *The Rise of the Creative Class*, argues that creativity will be the main skill of workers in the 21st-century marketplace. The times when most people worked in production or service are coming to an end—machines and computers do more and more of those jobs every day. Instead, the skills required from us in increasing measure are innovation and creativity.

This is especially true for people in cities. Edward Glaser argues in his book *Triumph of the City* that almost all innovation in the world comes from urban centers. There are several reasons for this (density, diversity, experts, the arts), but the relevance of having creative and innovative skills is even more important in cities than anywhere else. Because more and more people are living in cities, innovative skills have become more and more crucial.

Creativity is even more important for people in the startup scene—people who are starting a business, a non-profit, a new initiative, or planting a church. They have to be able to think outside of the box and create new projects, models, programs, and ministry expressions. They must be good at troubleshooting, contextualizing, and learning from mistakes, rather than simply acting as agents of continuity or tradition. If they lead organizations, businesses, or churches, they can't just be innovators—they must also be innovation *leaders*. They need to know how to stimulate creativity not only in themselves, but in those they lead.

When my family and launch team moved to Frankfurt in 2009 to plant a new church, we were twelve young believers with a vision: start a church for people in Frankfurt who wanted nothing to do with the church or Christian faith. Previously, we were all members of existing churches where things were done the way they always had been done. Changing something was always a challenge. But now we were in a church plant.

We spent eighteen months learning to understand our context and planning what our new church would look like. Innovation was crucial to us. We tried to be as creative as possible. We brainstormed, visualized, storyboarded, conducted studies. We asked people in Frankfurt what a church they would go to would look like. For most team members, this was new. As a leader, I not only had to think creatively, but I also had to lead an innovative team and stimulate creativity in everyone around me. Later, when the church gained momentum, a friend said to me, "You have a very creative church."

I took that as a compliment.

Urban church planters in the 21st century are, by definition, innovators. Creative skills are crucial to their task. This means City to City is a movement of urban innovators. We need to understand the importance of creativity and have the skills to stimulate and lead innovation in order to see movements of the gospel in the cities of Europe.

Who Is Creative?

The normal response I get when talking to people about creativity is, "I am not the creative type." The idea they are expressing is that some people are born creative and have innovation in their DNA, while others do not. But is that so? I want to challenge that idea with two perspectives—one educational and one biblical.

Educational Perspective

In his book *Out of Our Minds*, Ken Robinson argues that our schools are not built to develop creativity because they were designed for an industrial age. As a result, learning mostly means memorizing content or doing things correctly, and the creative subjects like painting, dance, or poetry are deemphasized. Since most education does not support and stimulate creativity, many people don't think of themselves as creatives. But the opposite is true.

Pablo Picasso said, "All children are born artists. The problem is to remain an artist when we grow up." It is amazing how much creativity kids have. They are comfortable with fantasy and have the freedom to play, to imagine, to try and fail, to learn, to dream, and to test everything. Children are born creative—my own four-year-old son proves that every day. Take all electronic devices away and leave him alone in his room; he turns into Batman, fights the Joker with a superweapon, and saves the world. We may call it chaos, but in the end, it is true creativity. And everybody is born with it. All humans have creative capacity, even if they don't think they do.

Biblical Perspective

Christian ideas about God, the world, and humans are very positive about creativity. God himself claims the name "Creator." And he *created* humans as innovative *creatures* in an environment that has maximum potential for innovation.

1. The source of creativity

At the beginning of the Bible, God presents himself as the Creator of the universe. He designed the heavens and the earth. He imagined all of the plants and animals and breathed them into existence. He designed chemistry, biology, medicine, DNA, time, and natural laws. Like a painter, he brought amazing galaxies, beautiful mountains, colorful flowers, and tasty fruits to life. Out of nothing, he made the sun and the moon. And at the culmination of it all, he created man and woman in his image. God is the most creative being of all. Creativity is obviously one of his attributes. That is why so much beauty exists in the world—our God is an artist.

In faith, we pray to the Creator of the universe. We have a direct, personal connection to the source of creativity—the one who is creativity himself. Just as a piece of art reflects the artist, the world mirrors its Creator in beauty and ingenuity. As children of God, we are like the kids of the most famous artist of the world.

When we think about how to learn, stimulate, and lead with creativity, our connection to the source of creativity—our God—may be unexpectedly helpful.

2. *The call to creativity*

In Genesis 2, God calls the man he has just created to join him in the process of innovation; God gives him the task of naming all the animals. Picture this scene: there are thousands of animals waiting in line. God pulls up chairs for himself and Adam, gets a notebook and a pen and says, "Okay. Now it's on you. Tell me their names!"

And Adam begins. The first species comes forward. "Elephants."

"Alright, next one."

"Eagles."

And so it goes on for hours.

One of the first things God taught our forefather was to be creative. God could have given Adam a list of the animals' names, but his desire was for humans to join him in the creative process. And that was only the beginning. God put Adam and Eve on a whole planet full of raw materials teeming with incredible potential. Today, thousands of years later, we are still discovering new aspects of this creation. God could have had it all finished—technology, medicine, science—but he didn't. Especially in our age, when the revealed potential that God bestowed upon nature is so enormous, the idea that God wanted us to be creative is obvious. God called humans to be creative from the beginning. And that is still one of our callings.

For many centuries, the family of God, the Church, was a main supporter of and venue for creativity and art. Much of Europe's rich cultural history (Michelangelo's paintings, Bach's music) emerged in and around the church. As Christians, we use creativity and art to praise our God by singing songs, building amazing cathedrals, and creating other works of art and praise. Anyone who has ever walked into Antoni

Gaudi's Sagrada Familia cathedral in Barcelona or listened to one of Bach's concertos has experienced an example of creativity used to glorify God.

What Is the Problem with Creativity?

There are many factors that can limit or hinder our creative potential—traditional paradigms tell us that things have to be done the way they have always been done. Pragmatism that puts efficiency above all other values allows no time to be creative. Lack of resources restricts the freedom necessary for innovation. Add to this most leaders' lack of awareness and inability to stimulate creativity. But even if you remove all of those other limitations, there is one more that kills almost all creativity: the fear of failure.

To be creative, we need the freedom to explore, dream, and test new ideas. Only in an environment that encourages us to try, fail, and try again can we learn new things and to innovate. While inventing the light bulb, Thomas Edison made hundreds of mistakes. Later, he said, "I didn't fail a thousand times. The light bulb was an invention with a thousand steps." However, the fear of failure or the paradigm of perfection can kill creativity. If we always play it safe, we never come up with something new.

As a German, I know this quite well. Germans are known for their high standards. This is why "made in Germany" is a quality guarantee recognized worldwide. But the reason for this is actually that we are afraid to fail. There is not much risk-taking or innovative potential in our culture. In fact, we professionalized this fear so much that it became a technical term—the so-called German *Angst* (the German word for "fear"). To be and to stay creative is a challenge, especially in environments with an intense pressure to succeed.

A multitude of voices speak this creativity-killing paradigm of fear into our lives. Here are three:

The Teacher

The first person who teaches us to avoid failure is our teacher. Ken Robinson points out that our whole education system is built on the motivation to avoid failure. Teachers train kids to do everything correctly. Through our whole education, we learn that the best grades are given to the ones who make no mistakes. If you succeed in school, you are groomed to be a no-mistake professional.

Church planters are often educated theologians trained by religious experts and teachers. In the more conservative wings of theological education, the fear of heresy and the desire to be right can become innovation killers. Of course, there is great value in good, solid theology. A sound and detailed understanding of the gospel is crucial. But theological perfectionism, which can become a legalistic fear of failure, is an innovation killer. There was not a lot of creativity amongst the Pharisees, but the early church, driven by the gospel of the freedom of Christ, was a movement filled with innovation.

The Boss

When we leave school and enter our professional work lives, the next person who tells us to make no mistakes is our boss. Not every boss is like this, but many jobs create an atmosphere where mistakes are not seen as positive. Innovative companies like Google or Yahoo give their workers a significant amount of time to try new things and make mistakes, and they are celebrated for it, but this form of leadership is still not the rule.

In the church planting world, the expectations of some denominational leaders, donors, and mentors of what it looks like to "succeed" pose a real challenge. The expectation of moral perfection, goals for the growth of the church plant, or basic expectation to raise enough funds for your project can lead to paralyzing fear of failure. It extinguishes the innovative spark a church planter needs. Of course, there need to be goals and boundaries, but innovators also need the space to be creative. Urban church planters need an environment with enough healthy freedom to be innovators.

So, our teachers tell us to avoid failure during our education, our boss does the same at our job, and on top of this comes:

The Pastor

His message is often the same: do no wrong! Live a good, moral life that pleases God. If you do so, you will be blessed and welcomed by God. This message—sadly, often the message of the church—leads to fundamentalist traditionalism and adds to the voices that make us fearful of failure.

I don't want to be misunderstood. I appreciate teachers and think they do a great job. There are many gentle and fair bosses in the world. And I am a pastor myself. But it is important to see that the way we run our schools, companies, and churches may hinder creativity rather than encourage it.

We need a voice that helps us deal with failure differently and counteract the narratives of fear. What can help us?

How the Gospel Makes Us More Creative

There are many strategies to help people experience freedom to try, fail, and keep trying. Many of the young tech companies and entrepreneur hubs do a good job of stimulating creative thinking in their workers by giving them freedom to start a project that may not even work out in the end.

But the fear of failure is often a deeper, more personal struggle. It is connected to our self-worth, our desires for security and approval, and, oftentimes, our concept of spirituality. If my fear of failure is not only a matter of getting time at work to invent new apps or products but is more deeply rooted in my personal need not to lose face (or my salvation!), then a more fundamental freedom is needed.

The Christian faith is often viewed—by both Christians and non-Christians—as a religion about keeping moral laws so that God might bless us, answer our prayers, and welcome us to heaven one day. Sadly, this perception of Christianity is based on experience. The message of perfectionism is one people often hear in churches, but it is not the original idea of the Christian faith. It is not the unique message of Jesus Christ. It is not the gospel.

The gospel says that God sent us his son, who lived the perfect life and died for all our imperfections on the cross. He promised that if we believe in him, this perfection will be ours, too. We aren't required to live a sinless life out of guilt or to build a moral record that our lives depend upon. God will not judge us by what we have done or the mistakes we have made. Because of what his son has done for us, we are free.

The grace of the gospel frees us from the fear of failure. If we fail—whether our innovative project doesn't work or we mess up in our personal lives—we don't have to be afraid; Jesus has already lived and died for us. This gives us the freedom to try as hard as we can and fail. And when we experience failure, the gospel gives us ways to handle it—repentance, forgiveness, and redemption. Through the gospel, we can overcome the fear of failure and have the courage to be creative.

The gospel in itself is a very innovative thing. Through Jesus, God created a whole new way for faith and relationship with God to function. In every other worldview, philosophy, or religion, our job as humans is to try to be good on our own. When Jesus came, died, and rose again, he changed that completely. He called it a new covenant. On the cross, Jesus created something that has never been seen before: the gospel. God's greatest invention of all time. The Creator's best creation. The most beautiful work of art by the greatest artist. And it started the most successful start-up of all time: the church.

What Helps Us Be Creative?

If we are called to be creative and the gospel gives us the freedom to do so, what are practical ways to be innovative? Here is a short collection of practices to grow our creativity:

Play

In one *Star Trek* movie, Data, an android whose purpose is to become as human as possible, lands on a new planet and becomes friends with a little boy. However, Data is impatient with the boy because he spends his time playing around, not focusing on the mission. The boy responds to Data's frustration perfectly: "How can you try to become human without ever taking time to just play?" What we call "play" is children's language for trying new things without a purpose. Playing means to imagine and experiment. As adults, we have left the practice of playing behind because we are so focused on attaining our goals. But to play is to stimulate creativity.

Be Inspired

To be creative, take time to observe other creative innovators. Go to the opera, climb a mountain, sit on a river bank, watch the birds, go to a museum. However you do it, seek inspiration.

Cooperate

There are moments in a creative process where we have to be alone, thinking, imagining, and making up our mind. However, it also helps if we don't use just our own minds, but combine them with others and collaborate.

Diversify

In a creative process, it is not good to work *only* with people who are like us. The more diverse a group is on many levels (gender, profession, worldview, experience, age, social milieu, or personality), the more it will inspire innovation—if the cooperation works well.

Copy and Collect

Creativity often does not entail doing something completely new but instead combining what already exists in a new way. Therefore, it is a helpful practice to collect ideas, pictures, thoughts, or anything else that we find interesting.

Some may use an old fashioned notebook, others an app, but to have a place to collect creative ideas is important.

Meditate

Many innovators and artists have found creativity in meditation. Spirituality is very useful for creativity. It says a lot that the word "inspiration" stems from the same word as "spirit." In faith, we have access to God, the source and power for creativity, and many artists have expressed that their true inspiration comes from the Creator they worship and experience in meditation.

Try and Fail

As we've said, an atmosphere that has the freedom to try and fail and try again is essential to creativity. The process of discovering what works and what doesn't is every bit as valuable as the finished product you are working towards. Allow yourself the space to fail, and then keep going.

Stop

To make room for innovation, it is often crucial to stop doing something old. If we always do the same things in the same way, we will never create. It's like playing with Legos with my kids. We build a whole city with houses, cars, planes, and parks. But once all pieces are used, the only way to build something new is to deconstruct the old buildings. In many situations, the only way to innovate is to end something that exists. That can be painful but is often necessary.

Celebrate

Encourage and support creativity by celebrating it. Even if there is no big result or success, creativity in and of itself must be applauded. Only in an atmosphere where innovation is celebrated will people feel free to take risks.

These are some ways to stimulate creativity. There are many more—find healthy practices that work for you. It is good to invest and be intentional in how we train the creative capacity in ourselves and in others.

A friend of mine, Jason Holm, was creative in the way he planted his church in Cologne. Cologne is known for its tasty beer, its lively carnival, and the amazing cathedral in its center. The Catholic Church is not only visually present but part of the whole culture of the city. It is a city of many artists, and Jason is a painter himself.

When Jason planted a church in Cologne, he didn't start with the normal contemporary evangelical programs, such as a Sunday service with a great worship band and a kids ministry. After engaging with a lot of Colognians, he used their input to shape the way he designed his service. Their worship style is a much more liturgical, high church service with jazz music instead of mainstream contemporary Christian music. He often wears a hoodie with an appliqué, resembling a monks attire. As the work grew, he opened an art gallery where he has an office, but he also paints and takes time to talk with people. He invites other people to join him. And it fits Cologne in an innovative way.

If we want to see new and developed movements of the gospel in the cities of Europe, we will need a great deal of creativity to make it happen. The path forward is not dictated to us by God. He, the Creator himself, is able to inspire creativity in us and lead us to see what a movement of the gospel is: innovation.

Chapter 2

At the Intersection of Faith and Culture

A Vision for Christian Cultural Expressiveness

RENÉ BREUEL

We've started a new church. Now what?

This "what" should include, of course, nurturing this congregation: to teach the scriptures, disciple new believers, and train leaders. For us at Hopera Church in Rome, Italy, it also meant mentoring other church planters, starting daughter congregations, and laying the groundwork for a network of new churches in Italian cities. As we strove to accomplish these goals over the past few years, part of me enjoyed the organizational development, the backstage work, and seeing our church members grow as we met their needs.

But the church planter inside of me rebelled. I mean, come on—to live among Christians is thrilling, but what about that fascinating mess of a culture around us? Will we lose contact with the non-Christians who got us into church planting in the first place? *No sir*, I told myself. We will continue to be a church for non-Christians. We will help our people grow, and help them see that growth involves seeking the welfare of our city.

This essay tells the story of our church plant's attempts to engage non-Christians in Rome. It articulates a vision for cultural expressiveness, provides examples of concrete initiatives, and examines the convictions that nurture this vision—all in hopes of inspiring others to attempt their own humble exercises of culture making.

1

For me, the journey started with recognizing the limitations of the theological vision that used to guide me. The story of faith I inherited often started with human sin (Genesis 3) and finished with Jesus' sacrifice on the cross (Matthew 27 and parallels). To understand salvation as forgiveness for personal sins is certainly at the heart of the gospel. But if we stay there, we can unintentionally encourage an individualistic, separatist version of Christianity. This view has much to say about the heart and family, but little about work and wider society. It thrives on Sundays, but has little to do with Mondays. As a result, the books, songs, and art Christians produce are usually aimed at convinced Christians. When we try to speak to those who do not believe, those efforts usually take place on our turf and on our terms: evangelistic sermons, apologetic talks, and training for personal evangelism. We accept a privatized role, speaking to individual issues with religious services in a secular society.

But the biblical story is wider. It starts before human sin with creation (Genesis 1), and proceeds to Jesus' resurrection, ascension, and future renewal of all things (Revelation). It gives us a cultural mandate besides the Great Commission. It teaches us to seek the welfare of the city, not just our tribe (Jeremiah 29). It portrays Jesus healing bodies and saving souls and God's new creation of a garden-city where the Tree of Life is surrounded by the best of redeemed human culture. It encourages us to pursue movements of the gospel in our hearts, in our churches, *and* in our cities.

What could this look like? Authors have coined phrases like a "public faith," a "new Christian renaissance," or being a "creative minority" to describe believers who seek to contribute to the common good.[3] Perhaps the most helpful term for this lifestyle is Andy Crouch's suggestion: "culture making." According to Crouch's taxonomy in *Culture Making,* a disengaged minority usually consumes culture, condemns culture, and critiques culture. It complains about popular movies, music, and politics, but it does not do much beyond complaining and talking to itself. Such a minority may also copy culture and create a subculture for itself—with, say, Christian music, films, and books—but it is not audible beyond its own networks and Sunday gatherings. Crouch proposes a fifth posture beyond consuming, condemning, critiquing, and copying culture: we can also *create* culture. Culture making is not just a return to God's original plan for humankind to be gardeners who tend to his creation. It also contributes to culture in a way that consumption and condemnation can't. "The only way to change culture is to create more of it," writes Crouch. "Consequently, cultural change will only happen when something new displaces, to some extent, existing culture in a very tangible way."[4]

Notice the words "displaces" and "tangible ways." A good Christian book on explicitly religious and personal issues—say, prayer or marriage—won't displace romantic comedies, science fiction novels, or hip-hop songs. Christians need to write books on prayer and marriage *and* craft comedies, novels, and songs intended not just for fellow believers, but for the general public, as well. They need to tell stories that refract, apply, and point to the Great Story not just in sermons, but in movies, novels, songs, sculptures, poetry, academia, street art, and more. As one observer puts it, "Narrative is our culture's currency; he who tells the best story wins."[5] My conviction is that the story of Jesus' renewal of all things is the best story around. Are we telling it? I think we are. But are we telling it only to ourselves?

"The Christian faith malfunctions when it is practiced as a mystical religion in which ascent is followed by a *barren* rather than creative return, a return that has no positive purpose for the world," writes Miroslav Volf.[6] "Creative return" requires the confidence that we have something worthy to say. At the same time, we are called to give "a reason for the hope" inside us "with gentleness and respect" (1 Peter 3:15). We do so not to pursue power, but to humbly serve the common good. In the words of painter Makoto Fujimura, "Culture is not a territory to be won or lost but a resource we are called to steward with care. *Culture is a garden to be cultivated.*"[7]

Addressing the mainstream public instead of our religious subculture is a hard task. It means shedding the authority we use to teach those faithful and willing to be taught. Instead, as people "without authority," we strive to study and address the questions of today instead of our intramural debates, to interact with others on equal terms in the marketplace of ideas, and to craft cultural artifacts that stand on their own. In Jonathan Sacks' description, "To become a creative minority is not easy because it involves maintaining strong links with the outside world while staying true to your faith, seeking not merely to keep the sacred flame burning but also to transform the larger society of which you are a part. This is a demanding and risk-laden choice."[8]

To be a culturally expressive minority is a social role that many evangelicals aren't accustomed to playing. It means, for instance, envisioning the church not just as the gathered church, but also the scattered church, made by the contributions of both the clergy and those in other walks of life. It means understanding church planting not only as the formation of worshipping communities, but as broadcasting communities. It means understanding evangelism not only as bringing people in, but as releasing people of all vocations to tell stories that point, directly or indirectly, to Christ's story.

2

This is an inspiring vision. But what can our underfunded and understaffed band of brothers and sisters actually accomplish? Not everything—but not nothing either. At our church, we experimented along the intersection of faith and culture with initiatives aimed at helping people share their stories, compare stories, hear the gospel creatively, and broadcast their stories to the world.

1. Share Your Story in Seeker Groups

Our humble attempts at cultural engagement in Rome started with what we call *Gruppi Scoprire*. These "seeker groups" consist of a series of dinners that evolve into discussions about spiritual matters. During a group's first meeting, we ask everyone to introduce themselves and narrate their spiritual journey up to that point.

I stand amazed at these seekers' stories. For many, it's the first time in years they've reflected about spiritual matters. They don't know if they believe or not, *what* they believe in, if they *want* to believe, or what prompts them to keep coming. On one occasion, a young man told us that he was there just to please his mom, but he came back again and wanted to meet for coffee. A couple explained that they had searched for God for years, only to find lifeless liturgy. Now they are happy to catch glimpses of him, even if they don't fully see yet.

The group evolves into discussions of faith as we study episodes of the gospels over the course of a few weeks. By the time we reach Jesus' encounter with Nicodemus in John 3, their eyes sparkle at the possibility of being born again. And I watch in awe, delighting in this microcosm of encounter between belief and unbelief.

2. Comparing Stories in Debates and Conversations

The next step in our congregational experiment in cultural engagement involved organizing debates with representatives of other religious viewpoints. We first invited the Italian Union of Atheists and Rationalistic Agnostics to two debates about the existence of God at a local university. I was surprised at how easy people found it to invite friends to these events. It was a step of growth for us, too, to hold events that did not proclaim our perspective alone, on our turf and in our terms, but interacted with another worldview on public grounds and in equal terms. We then held debates with leaders of the largest Buddhist group in Italy on the meaning of life and with a representative of the Mosque of Rome on how religion can be a force for peace in the world today. Each of these opportunities allowed us to build respectful friendships with these groups. It brought us in contact with individuals who then started to explore Christianity. And it helped us see that ours is a *public* gospel: good news for everyone.

A more advanced version of this experiment has been held by Tiago Cavaco at *Igreja da Lapa* in Lisbon, Portugal. A few years ago, he started hosting entire weekends of conversations. The edition I got to see (I was so curious that I flew there to check it out myself) featured a conversation between left-wing and right-wing congressmen on how people can disagree civilly, panels on abortion rights and how evangelicals are perceived by Portuguese society, and interviews with a member of the Portuguese House of Representatives, a nationally-known singer, and a disabled woman. It was fascinating. Tiago told me that, for many speakers and audience members alike, it was their first time in an evangelical church.

3. Tell the Gospel Story Creatively with Cultural Artifacts and Events

In addition to cerebral, discourse-heavy debates, we tried to host artistic events that spoke primarily to the heart and to the imagination. Some involved simply encouraging and attending events like music concerts, photography exhibits, and plays held by artists in our church. Others were events our church sponsored. For example, we joined forces with a student ministry and other churches to put on the Mark Drama, a theatrical portrayal of the gospel of Mark. On the International Day of Women, we supported *Caradonna*, an exhibit featuring photos of women for women, which led to intriguing conversations. *Aperitivo* evenings with music, food, and short talks have also been a popular format. One night, we encouraged people to craft small objects that made them reflect on what they believe and take them home or gift them to someone.

Then, there were unplanned developments we couldn't have imagined. One of these started when a couple—he a contemporary art director, she a singer—came to faith a few years ago. They started witnessing to their company members and friends, and a dozen of them—rappers, actors, dancers—came to faith in Christ. The play they produce each year has now become a catalyst for our witness. Using unconventional devices like the displacement of the public—who, according to their responses, may or may not see Jesus' resurrection at the end of the play—provokes questions for non-Christians. They also provoke long-time Christians who, accustomed to a written and preached gospel, have never imagined their faith being communicated by a surreal, theatrical storyline.

4. Help People Broadcast Stories to the World

The confluence of these efforts has encouraged us to consider initiating an artists' collective. In a sense, our church already functions as a hub to gather and empower professionals of all vocations. But we've been reflecting on how we can "scatter" and intentionally contribute to the common good as we meet together and hear from God. Such a collective could take the form of "vocational fellowships"—for entrepreneurs, scientists, etc.—that Redeemer Presbyterian Church and other churches in New York offer for professionals to reflect about their work in light of the Christian faith.[9] It could take a form similar to *Sputnik Magazine*, a British network that connects, challenges, and funds Christian artists who want to share their creative skills with people outside of the church. At the moment, we're still in the envisioning phase.

3

To be Christians who contribute to the common good is not without challenges. How can we sustain these efforts in the face of obstacles?

Navigate Working in and for Multiple Audiences

A first challenge is the emotional dissonance that results from using various disciplines, genres, and languages to speak to multiple audiences. Will folks lend an ear to explicitly Christian voices? Should our art be like our sermons and always lead to Jesus? Is it okay if faith is not made explicit? And if we want to bring our faith into our work, where will it fit? Makoto Fujimura, a painter at home in both secular galleries and Christian environments, writes that "Life on the borders of a group—and in the space between groups—is prone to dangers literal and figurative, with people both at home and among the 'other' likely to misunderstand or mistrust the motivations, piety, and loyalty of the border-stalker."[10] Similarly, Alan Jacobs, in an essay on the challenges of Christian intellectuals, confesses that,

> *I have felt for my entire career the difficulties of deciding where to speak and how. About a decade into my professional life it suddenly dawned on me that...I was never going to have a single audience. It would be necessary for me at times to speak to the church; at other times to believers from other religious traditions; at other times to my fellow academics; and at yet other times to the American public at large.... I would have to strive to be, as the Apostle Paul said, all things to all people, however disorienting and puzzling that obligation might be.[11]*

Our churches should also accept that we address multiple audiences and encourage members to do the same. For instance, instead of judging works of art as if they were theological treatises, we need to extend thinkers and artists the grace to craft works that respect the aims of a project, the composition of its intended audience, and the conventions of the genre. Some cultural artifacts may just raise questions. Some may be protests against societal evils. Some may bear explicit witness to faith in Christ. Some may address a wide audience, some believers, some a specific niche or tribe, and some a mixed audience. Many may originate from a Christian institution such as a church or religious publisher, others from festivals, producers, publishers, or magazines of no religious conviction. Yet all of these can be works of excellence that enrich the common good in infinite ways.

Thinking Long-Term

To release cultural artifacts into mainstream culture is hard work, of course. Artists, thinkers, and other professionals need years to study, experiment, and attempt several unsuccessful projects. It takes conviction and encouragement to persevere in crafts that take time to be mastered. But if we don't work past failed attempts, we may never run into a fruitful one. I try to think long-term in my own attempts to write books and articles for non-Christians. My unsuccessful experiments so far include an unpublished memoir about becoming a father and an aborted historical novel. At the moment, I'm working on a comedy screenplay for the Italian cinema. There may not be interest to produce it, but hope springs eternal—

who knows? We only find out by trying. If rejected, I'll count it a step forward in the "failed experiments" department.

A related challenge is that in secularized societies such as ours, people who wrestle with questions about faith will likely find larger audiences among and receive greater appreciation from fellow Christians in Christian gatherings. Outside audiences will probably be smaller, more skeptical, harder to speak to, and offer more rejection than recognition. Christian communities should be hubs of encouragement along the way—giving space for early experiments, showing up for half-empty launches and opening nights—and bless professionals who try to speak in other settings.

We may often address our fellow believers, of course. But like missionaries to a foreign land, we may also want to invest years in learning new languages, sacrifice the comforts of our emotional home, and pursue a more difficult road as missionaries to the culture.

A Call to Faithful Culture Making

We don't need to accept the terms of secularism. Nor should we limit ourselves to announcing the hope of Christ only within our walls. We can plant movements of urban churches that contribute to the spiritual, social, and cultural flourishing of our cities. We can empower believers to scatter and serve the common good in all vocations and areas of society. "Let a thousand flowers bloom," wrote William Wilberforce to encourage a generation of Christians who helped abolish the slave trade and pursue greater justice and compassion through various causes.[12]

I say we have a lot more planting, gardening, and blooming to do.

Chapter 3

Integral Life

*Building Multi-Ethnic
Christian Communities*

JURJEN TEN BRINKE

Introduction

I will never forget the time in my church when a Turkish sister asked forgiveness of some young Kurdish men. Because of the conflict between the Kurdish, who don't have their own state, and the Turks, there is a lot of political tension between these groups. But the gospel changed this woman, so she desired justice for these Kurdish refugees. She asked their forgiveness and literally washed their feet.

I also think of the Iranian Muslims who, while waiting for political asylum, helped decorate our church for Christmas. They came just because we asked them to help—to be a part of the community of believers who know God or want to know him better. They quickly became friends with people from our church. They encountered the Good News just by being acknowledged for their unique abilities and qualities, whether they already believed in God or not.

Amsterdam, where I live and minister, is one of the most multi-ethnic cities in the world with approximately 180 nationalities living there. However, our city's churches are most often "black" or "white." Dozens of migrant churches (Ghanaian, Nigerian, Egyptian, or Indonesian) are present in the city, but they mainly reach people in their own culture. Within mainstream white churches (made up mostly of people born in Christian families), most migrants feel like strangers. While our schools, universities, sporting clubs, and public transport are mixed communities in which many different people meet each other, our churches are organized in a way that reinforces separation. Does this mean a multi-ethnic church is just a dream?

It is possible, if we choose, to be an inclusive church in which multi-ethnicity is not a threat but an inviting challenge. But we must choose to live an "integral life" in which spirit, soul, and body are all important. We must choose to always look for God's image in other people and desire for it to come to fruition. We do this with the hope that people will meet the Lord Jesus, so that the gospel can change them from the inside out. The result can be a wonderful community that gives us a taste of God's kingdom, where people from all tongues and cultures will stand together before God's throne in eternity (Revelation 7:9).[13]

Theology and Chances of Being a Multi-Ethnic Church

The Bible gives us many guidelines for interaction between cultures. Although the origin of cultures is still subject to discussion (i.e., are the consequences of the Tower of Babel in Genesis 11 a blessing or a curse?), it is clear throughout scripture that God's greatness is visible in the diversity of his church, the body of Christ with its many parts. There are even biblical reasons to maintain ethnic differences in the church of Jesus Christ.[14] Let me mention a few.

1. *The community God is building is "a school of Christ"*

In Ephesians 3:18-19, Paul says: "[I pray that] you may have power, together with all the saints, to grasp how wide and long and high and deep is the love of Christ, and to know this love that surpasses knowledge that you be filled to the measure of all the fullness of God."

In order to know Christ's fullness, we need all the saints. Only together and in the power of the Holy Spirit can we discover the four-dimensional glory of Christ—its length, width, height, and depth. Other cultures show us new perspectives on scripture. For example, Western Europeans usually view the Bible through the glasses of a "debt-culture," which means they understand that Jesus came to earth to pay the debt caused by our sin. Middle-Eastern cultures, by contrast, see the scriptures through the lens of a "shame-culture," which means they emphasize that Jesus died mainly to cover their shame. Other cultures can also model different ways of worshiping and walking with God. The way Africans seem to have endless inner happiness and praise God at their all-night prayer groups shows a deep dependency on their Creator and reminds me how a disciple of Jesus should truly live. Ultimately, my theological view of the gospel is enriched through contact with believers of other cultures.

2. Walls of separation are broken down

Paul discusses how Jesus destroyed the division between Jew and Gentile concretely in Ephesians 2:14-18:

> *For he himself is our peace, who has made the two groups one and has destroyed the barrier, the dividing wall of hostility, by setting aside in his flesh the law with its commands and regulations. His purpose was to create in himself one new humanity out of the two, thus making peace, and in one body to reconcile both of them to God through the cross, by which he put to death their hostility. He came and preached peace to you who were far away and peace to those who were near. For through him we both have access to the Father by one Spirit.*

The early church consisted of both Jews and Greeks, which caused problems indeed (Acts 6:1). But the apostles didn't avoid these problems because they knew Jesus had broken down the wall between Jew and Gentile. Jesus also tore down the walls within the hearts of the Gentiles, and reconciled them to each other. An intercultural church is therefore the place where walls between Christians of Gentile descent (which is most of us) should be broken down.

In Amsterdam, many people avoid and neglect each other simply because their worlds are "too different." Within a multi-ethnic church, however, it is simply impossible to neglect each other. We confess the same dependency on the same Almighty God and the sacrifice of Jesus—we are *all* connected. I have seen a working class woman become a house cleaner for a wealthy migrant family in Amsterdam. They became friends and supported each other. Their common ground is the gospel of Jesus Christ.

3. Sharing the gospel

We create space within our church for migrants to share the gospel in their own language and with their own customs. As soon as we find a person from a specific cultural background who is able to lead a group, we start a "house church." Currently, we have a Persian house church (with Iranians and Afghans), a Kurdish house church, a Pakistani/Indian house church (with Urdu and Hindi languages), an African group, and a Surinamese group. These groups gather during the week to share their own food, music, customs, and language. They then join as one during Sunday worship services (conducted in Dutch, with headphone translation to English). Through house churches, we are able to reach communities that, otherwise, we would never be able to access in the right way—the house churches' leaders know and are part of their culture, speak their language, and have the sensitivity to deal with their way of life. The members can then take the gospel to their home countries during holidays or phone calls with family members. This calls to mind Jesus' words on spreading the faith to people of all cultures:

> *Then Jesus came to them and said, "All authority in heaven and on earth has been given to me. Therefore, go and make disciples of all nations, baptizing them in the name of the Father and of the Son and of the Holy Spirit, and teaching them to obey everything I have commanded you. And surely, I am with you always, to the very end of the age." —Matthew 28:18-19*

To celebrate this diversity corporately, our church has "cultural Sundays," which I plan together with our house church leaders. On a "Pakistani Sunday," I might wear Pakistani clothing, which empowers the Pakistanis to display their own culture in our congregation and makes them more comfortable to invite their friends to church. We might have an African offering during an "African Sunday," and all of the attendees bring their tithe to the front while African brothers and sisters in traditional dress play their culture's music.

Personal connections with people outside our usual circles influence how we prepare sermons and function as a church in our community. The unity of such a variety of people is visible to everyone around, including non-Christians. An intercultural church is God's special masterpiece. It is an apologetic that validates the truth of the gospel.

However, in our multicultural society, ministering amid diversity is difficult. All of Europe's countries are dealing with a migration crisis. There is also a growing gap between poor and rich, especially in big cities. Diversity is therefore not just about ethnic differences. It is also about socio-economic differences. In a time of growing division, the church can be a place to connect people who do not belong to the same ethnic group or social circles but who find each other tied together by the gospel of Jesus Christ.[15]

In our church, it hasn't been necessary to start a specific project like helping the poor. The home groups of our church in Amsterdam-Noord consist of people who are rich and people who are poor. They take care of each other, use each other's cars, cook for each other, and help each other in times of financial need. Although they aren't each other's *natural* peers and friends, this connection gives exactly what is missing in our individualistic society: the acknowledgment of each other's qualities and abilities within the body of Christ.

The different personalities and groups that form a church force us to be "formed and kneaded" until Christ's likeness becomes more visible in all of our lives (2 Corinthians 3:18).

At the same time, unity is experienced among them. As John Piper says,

> *God's great goal in all history is to uphold and display the glory of His name for the enjoyment of His people from all the nations. In step with God's great goal the Lord has allowed world migration today to bring many different peoples to the major cities. In the major metropolitan areas around the globe, intercultural churches are microcosms that simultaneously reflect a fulfilment of the Great Commission and foreshadow the reality of heaven.*[16]

Relationships and Living an Integral Life

If we want to anticipate the future, when the number of citizens from other cultural backgrounds will only grow, we must commit ourselves completely to building multicultural Christian communities.[17] Twelve years of church planting in Amsterdam and twenty years of spending time with asylum seekers have taught me this: building a multicultural church is impossible if the church planter and his team are unwilling to wholeheartedly invest in relationships with people from different cultures and social backgrounds. Organizing a multi-ethnic church without strong connections to other cultures can create a condescending "we do this for you" atmosphere in which there is no equality.[18] True friendship is essential. I remember when we organized a Christmas meal and an Afghan Muslim friend came in, bringing twelve (!) of his friends that I didn't know. During the break, I asked him why he brought his Muslim friends to our Christmas celebration. His answer was simple: "You're always connecting with me. Loving me. Respecting me. We share our lives and have fun together. If you organize a party, I'll be there with my friends, because you're my friend."

Like many others, I have had years of contradictory thoughts about the connection between evangelism and diaconal presence in my church's neighbourhood. In Amsterdam, I've seen churches with liberal theologies focused on social justice. I've seen evangelical churches focused mainly on contextualized worship services. I've seen conservative churches that preach only about saving your soul from hell. None of them have influenced the city significantly.

Several journeys to India, Uganda, and Iraq have made me realise that the perfect balance is found in the idea of **integral mission**. Integral mission means being a holistic church from which justice, peace, and joy flows into society. It is a kingdom-focused ministry. It means wanting to see Jesus, the Saviour from sin, be the Prince of Peace in every area of life. Thanks to integral mission, churches in the southern hemisphere seem to be more successful at being seen as a positive presence in society than many European churches. Of course, we must remember that secular Europe is totally different from spiritual Africa, but the lessons I learned from them turned out to be adaptable in Amsterdam's context.

1. Focus on the gifts God has already given you instead of what you feel is missing.

It can be tempting to worry about the gifts, talents, buildings, money, and, above all, church members that your church needs, but it is important to begin with thankfulness instead. A helpful biblical story to remember is the multiplication of bread and fish in Mark 6. One boy with just five loaves of bread and two fish put his belongings into the hand of Jesus, who performed a miracle with them. We have to learn to put what we have, even if we don't think it's enough, in the hands of Jesus. It was painful when I realised I learned this lesson from colleagues who are in much tougher situations than I am.

2. All Christians must live their Christian lives 24/7— especially the pastor.

Besides being a part of their church and participating in church events, all Christians have a responsibility to be active in their neighbourhood and publicly live out the Christian faith. This is true for pastors, too; are you pastoring just your church, or do you see yourself as a pastor of the neighbourhood, as well? Do you see yourself as a neighbour, a part of the community, even if your neighbours don't see you as one? Recognizing the importance of daily presence in our community made us realize that even the term "integral mission" might be too top-down. Mission sounds like something you go and do. Instead, we now talk about an **integral life**—a reality we live every day.

At Hope for North Church, we always stress that we have to *serve* each other instead of *help* each other. Serving means that we get involved in another person's life to walk with them as they flourish, rather than making them dependent on us. If a believer with a Muslim background is good at sports, let him teach me. If an Indian woman can cook well, let her serve us. The result is that, by serving, our members serve one another and everyone feels dignified.

3. The ultimate reason for integral life is to disciple the whole nation (whatever it looks like, exactly).

Some people are more comfortable with a Christian presence in their neighbourhood instead of people who "evangelize." However, as we live and serve in our neighborhoods daily, Christians need to maintain the conviction that a personal meeting with Jesus Christ himself is the very best thing that can happen in someone's life. If we miss that conviction, the risk of presenting a strictly social gospel is very high.

4. Integral life demonstrates God's Kingdom on earth.

Currently, there is a widespread desire for churches that exemplify what God's kingdom looks like—communities living life in all its fullness, free from poverty, injustice, and conflict. His kingdom is about proclaiming the good news to the poor, setting free those who are oppressed, and restoring the sight of the blind. The challenge for church leaders and planters is to journey toward the bigger goal of "shalom" (which, of course, is not just peace, but God's kingdom in everything). If we speak a message of transformation and shalom, then *we must live it*. If applying the truth of God's kingdom to our lives is the goal, we must throw off everything that hinders us and work toward it together. That work involves both the head (our rationale and theological understanding) and our heart (obedience, willingness, spiritual discernment, and emotional decision). It involves the hands, the eyes, and the community. As Luther said, we are God's hands and feet in this world that bring his peace.

Among others, Stefan Paas mentions the importance of not separating evangelism from other dimensions of mission.[19] His description of the classic model of *plantatio ecclesiae* shows that evangelism and the Christianization of society went hand in hand. Halfway through the nineteenth century, when all kinds of denominations sent missionaries across the globe, this ideal had been lost, and church planting became merely denominational expansion. The church, David Bosch says, ceased to point to God or to the future; instead, it was pointing to itself.[20] The relationship of these churches to society and the wider ecumenical and eschatological horizons was largely ignored.

We now have the chance to learn from this and to promote an inclusive way of being a kingdom-focused church again. Matthew 12:18 shows us what it means to see God's kingdom come and his will be done on earth as it is in heaven: "Behold my servant whom I have chosen, my beloved with whom my soul is well pleased. I will put my Spirit upon him, and he will proclaim justice to the Gentiles." Matthew quotes Isaiah, who states that Jesus came to bring liberty and justice. It is not just a fruit of the gospel—it *is* the gospel.

We can consider the refugee crisis as a practical example of the theology of integral mission.[21] Many Christians agree that we have a responsibility to take care of refugees, since Jesus explains in Matthew 25 that whoever receives a stranger in his house does this for Jesus himself. And although many of us have excellent ideas, talk about renewal during Sunday services, and reach out to people in our city, we must also take care of those coming to our cities as refugees. Some Christians call it a curse: Islam is taking over Europe. My guess is that they are wrong. Whatever God means with all of this, the world belongs to him! Even now, there are large numbers of refugees, including Muslims, on our doorsteps. We don't need to *take* them the kingdom through missions. We can *show* them the kingdom here. To do this, we have to engage them in sincere relationships.

If we do not participate in the lives of the people around us, we are working on projects rather than building the kingdom. We need to break down structures of injustice and proclaim the kingdom wherever possible. Just "helping refugees" is not an option. If we treat helping refugees as a project, we place them in a position of dependency and place ourselves in a position of self-satisfaction. Therefore, we can't just be a "helpful church"—we must bring justice as well as mercy. Justice means that none of us look down on others, that we break down the structures of racism. It even means breaking down the idea that we need to protect our self-built European welfare against those who threaten our prosperity. The gospel is about breaking down barriers—barriers between people (compare Peter and the gentile Cornelius) and the barrier between God and us. Broken barriers are evidence of God's work.

Living an integral life, then, means all our church members should be vessels of justice, breaking down whatever barriers stand in their surroundings.[22] Our Sunday worship services should function as a check-up service: build up your people to be lovers, peace-builders, and bringers of justice (instead of having just a nice, contextualized gathering of new believers). In our church, we offer people the opportunity to share what God has done in their life over the past week. Those short testimonies (told by Christian and non-Christian visitors alike) help people see how we can bring hope in our city, even if it starts on a small, personal scale.

In our case, we defined our vision for church planting as "helping the people of Amsterdam-Noord to be the light of Jesus Christ in their specific spot" (the vision was not *specifically* to plant a multi-ethnic church). If people come to Christ, or if Christians move into new neighbourhoods, we encourage them to be active in all kinds of committees and boards in the city: football, primary schools, neighbourhood committees, and so on. Living an integral life is a theological foundation, and indicates that God rules over all spheres of life. This is the kingdom that Jesus established and that we must continue. Our mission as followers of Jesus Christ must adequately reflect God's love for all creation.

Conclusion

The demographics of cities are always changing. In nearly every metropolitan area of Europe, there is a great diversity of cultures, nationalities, and social layers. The same is true in the United States and many other countries all over the world. In order to reach our cities with the gospel, then, we need to plant more churches that focus specifically on intercultural diversity. These churches should focus on multi-ethnic neighbourhoods and all socioeconomic classes, including Muslim immigrants and refugees.

The testimony of a church that unites the nations might even be greater when its diversifying society is perceived as a threat, not a challenge. For example, a church can show unification in a way no government could ever dream of. Intercultural church planting helps people integrate with their new home country. The various ethnic groups will get to know each other's cultural habits and learn to understand and respect each other in an open, God-loving environment.

Followers of Jesus need to be driven by the gospel, worship God, love their neighbours, and bring about social action and justice as an output of a God-inspired internal life. We must realise that the kingdom of God is expressed both inside and outside the church and share our lives with both Christians and non-Christians. Discipling the nations starts with an integral life as followers of Jesus who love their neighbours. As Dietrich Bonhoeffer explains, those who love their own dream of community will destroy the community. Those who love the people around them will create a community.[23]

Chapter 4

Developing Gospel-Shaped Social Businesses in the City

SEÁN MULLAN

And work for the peace and prosperity of the city where I sent you into exile.

– Jeremiah 29:7 (NLT)

This is the story of an idea shaped by the gospel, planted in a city, and grown into a business that generated social change. It is also an invitation to rethink the idea and rewrite the story in another city.

Beginning

In 2009, I left my job as pastor of a community church in a Dublin suburb after nine years. After twenty-two years as a professional church planter and church leader, I set out on a road I had never travelled with no income for the journey.

There were two ideas for my next steps: work with others to develop a gospel movement in Dublin, and start a hospitality business in the city centre. Both ideas took longer and proved harder than I hoped. But ignorance of the future is great protection when you set out on an adventure.

Three things influenced my thinking and motivation:

First, I wanted to be in the city. I had invited Tim Keller into my life, so I knew that the city is where people's ideas and values are shaped. I wanted to work in the city, not the suburbs.

Second, Dublin has a cultural suspicion of "professional religion." People may show superficial respect for a professional religious leader, but underneath there is a strong vein of distrust and even contempt. I saw value in being given a hearing as an amateur rather than a professional in the God conversations.

Third, I was convinced of the intangible power of good hospitality. People I know who never come to church and don't care for spiritual conversation are always ready to come to our table and spend hours at a meal. My wife Ana's excellent cooking skills and a half-decent bottle of wine have lowered many a guard and led to all kinds of wonderful conversations. I wanted to be in the business of practising hospitality.

From those three notions grew a social business called Third Space, which now operates a café in the centre of Dublin. It is run as a profit-generating business that also provides significant social benefit. It employs 25 people and offers food, drink, and a welcoming space to hundreds of people each week. It also provides practical and financial support for community groups, social projects, and creative bodies of many kinds. It is a centre of life and hospitality in the area. Its opening became a significant catalyst in the social renewal of its neighbourhood. And it is all shaped by the gospel notion that we do good to others because God has done good to us.

This paper explores the idea, "What would happen if Jesus' followers created social businesses?" It provides illustrations from Third Space's story. It reflects on what part these social businesses might play in a wider gospel movement in the city. Finally, it presents some possible next steps for you in your city.

What Is a Social Business?

Ordinary businesses exist to make a profit for investors. This profit becomes a dividend payment to the people who own the business. Apple is an ordinary business, as is your local convenience shop.

In contrast to business, charities exist to lose money for the sake of doing good. Most charities spend money raised from donors such as governments, philanthropists, businesses, and the general public. UNICEF is a charity, as is your local homeless shelter.

Social businesses are a third type of establishment—they make money while they work, but they don't do so to earn a dividend for their owners and investors. Instead, a social business exists to solve a social problem. It is, as Nobel Prize-winning economist Muhammad Yunus describes it, a "non-loss, non-dividend company dedicated entirely to achieving a social goal." One early example of a social business is a Bangladeshi yoghurt drink company set up by a local community bank and a multinational food business. The instigating problem was a lack of basic daily nutrition for children in Bangladesh. The solution was Grameen Danone, a business set up to design, produce, and sell a yoghurt drink containing all the daily nutrients needed for a child to grow healthily. They now sell 100,000 drinks a day and helped 250 women set up small businesses selling these drinks. The business may produce and sell yoghurt drinks, but the goal is overcoming children's malnutrition. A social business takes charity's desire to do good and business's capacity to create gain and merges them into a single entity.

Analysis and Questions

Dublin's Social Problem

The Third Space project sought to address one of Dublin's social problems exposed by the first boom and bust cycle of the 21st century. Before 2008, frenetic building development dominated the city. Countless apartments and offices were built. After the financial crash, many of these projects were left unfinished and city neighbourhoods were left disconnected and incomplete. No one considered how these new residents and workers would meet each other, connect to the existing community, and engage in the life of their neighbourhood. The need for a "third space"—a space that wasn't for living or working—was obvious. The neighborhood needed a space for locals to gather regularly, informally, and inexpensively.

"Tell me your thoughts about the city," was the line I used on local business owners, builders, city officials, activists, church leaders, police, and residents over coffee. As we talked, I learned that I wasn't alone in my analysis of the problem. Many agreed that the end product of the development process had not been good for the city. They also agreed that the notion of third places, local informal gathering places in redeveloped areas, was important.

Third spaces can take many forms—a bar or a barber shop, a laundrette or a library. We chose to begin with a café since it would be attractive to a wide cross section of the community. It would also fit the criteria of being local, regular, informal, and inexpensive. So the vision became a neighbourhood café run as a profitable business for the sake of regenerating a city neighbourhood. In early 2011, conversations with city officials and local people led us to decide on Smithfield, a redeveloped part of Dublin's legal quarter, as the venue for our social experiment. An enormous building project left unfinished by the economic crash seemed like ripe ground for sowing some social capital.

Theological Questions

As the social ideas developed, church friends began asking hard questions:

"What does this have to do with the gospel?"

"Is there any theological thinking behind this?"

"Will you evangelize in Third Space?"

The ensuing conversations centred on the damage of greed and the power of relationships. Greed had fueled the financial meltdown. Greed in the business and banking sectors did not just damage those sectors—the whole city was damaged. The Third Space project was an attempt to both mitigate the damage and help the city flourish.

The Third Space project is also about relationships. Our business plan supported the notion that loving one's neighbour is God's second great purpose for humanity. By creating both the space and the environment for neighborly relationshps to begin and grow, we sought to collaborate with that purpose. The plans and strategies that shaped Dublin had ignored that truth. Our project was an attempt to take it seriously.

While these goals became my theological defence of the project to the more sceptical of my church friends, they were never going to be enough to actually get something off the ground. That required a lot more conversations with a lot more people.

People, Money and Place

The Tribe

One outcome of these conversations was a large group of interested people. Over time, these formed into three circles of affinity. The inner circle was a group of workers. The middle circle was a group of advisors. The outer circle was a group of supporters. These three circles together formed the Third Space Tribe.

The inner team formed around me. My wife, Ana, was chief cheerleader and spiritual advisor. My friend Tim signed on because we had worked together in church leadership and he had a wealth of business experience. My sister Paula signed on because she was family, because we were close, and because she had a lifetime's experience in professional hospitality. And Conor, a student in a class I had taught, shared my passion for doing things differently. The fact that he was a highly experienced accountant also helped.

The inner circle helped to grow the other circles and draw others in with their enthusiasm. And this inner circle worked for no reward other than the joy of involvement. No funds meant no wages. Yet they worked hard, teaching me that people are motivated by the belief that they are doing good. I learned to believe that doing good was good *for* them, even if I couldn't reward their work.

Eventually, the right people working together produced a plan. It contained every element of a normal business strategy—market analysis, sales projections, growth predictions. The difference was our goal of tackling a social problem.

The Funds

Third Space was launched in 2011 in the middle of Ireland's financial crisis. The IMF was, effectively, in charge of the nation's finances. Banks were not lending anything to anyone. So, we approached potential funders with this request: lend us €5,000 or €10,000 to be repaid over five years, preferably at no interest. The people we approached were mainly part of the growing third circle, people we thought might have the funds and be well-disposed toward the project. We did not limit our request to people of faith. Our pitch had a wider appeal because it was about benefiting the city, not promoting the church. In the end, half of our investors were affiliated with a church. Half were not.

Many were intrigued by the request. Businessmen and women were used to being asked to invest in businesses or donate to charities. But they had never had a request like ours. Because the funds requested were relatively small, they did not see it as a major risk. Perhaps many of these people believed they would never see their money again and were surprised when repayments started to come in.

The Place

Third Space Smithfield finally opened its doors for business in February 2012. On the first day, it was packed with enthusiastic customers. Even though we were prepared and trained, the crowds overwhelmed us. Our coffee supplier had to roll up his sleeves and work for a few hours because he could see the team was struggling.

What appeared to be just a good first day became a good first week and a good first month. Marketing plans were abandoned as unnecessary—taking care of the customers already coming in became the priority. There was a high level of enthusiasm among these people for Third Space. There was an intense buzz in there each day.

Customers began speaking passionately about how "special" the place was. A woman told a staff member that there was a special word in Danish—*hule*—meaning a place of rest or refuge. "This is a *hule*," she said. Another regular said, "This place has a generous spirit and people need that right now." Yet another said the place made him feel like he was in his own kitchen.

On a dark evening the following winter, a customer called in to say how welcoming and warm the place looked as he walked up the square. He then came back, put his head through the door, and quietly said, "It's a wonderful thing you've done."

Another man, a security guard, came in one morning before the business was open. The café was empty except for one staff member who offered to make him a coffee. He walked around the space while he waited, and as he came to the counter, his normally serious expression had been replaced by a smile. "This is a very special place," he pronounced.

That word kept coming up: "special."

After we had been open for two years, Smithfield was a very different area. The senior city planner for the area called in and spoke of how much the area had changed. Two years before, Smithfield was a failed redevelopment. Businesses were closing or moving elsewhere. Now Smithfield is a major success, a thriving neighbourhood. The city planner thought Third Space had started that change. Soon after Third Space opened in Smithfield, someone tweeted, "I was going to leave Smithfield in September when my lease is up but @thirdspace has changed my mind."

Social and Theological Reflection

Measuring Social Impact

One of the challenges of running a social business is measuring its social benefit. Measuring financial impact is easy. Measuring social benefit requires ingenuity. A social business in India that sells soap to the unhygienic measures its social impact by the reduction of sick days for school children.

Measuring the social impact of Third Space is still a work in progress. However, some measurements are straightforward. We measure the number of jobs we provide, especially those for people deemed at risk of long-term unemployment. We also consider the staff's personal development. In addition to practical skills acquired on the job, the project has helped dozens of young people grow in personal confidence, teamwork, and interpersonal skills. We measure the people who move on from Third Space with better employment prospects than before.

Another aspect Third Space measures is the number of groups that have found a home in the café and use it for their own activities. Most of these groups are not-for-profits that provide significant social benefit, and the facilities at Third Space are an important support for them. One group runs a monthly event for newcomers to the city. Another is a vegetable co-operative connecting apartment dwellers directly to farmers in the countryside. Another group runs "philosophy cafés" where people gather to discuss life's big questions.

Dennis began to visit Third Space and fell in love with it. He was involved with the National Humanist Society, and since they were about to launch a new publication, he asked if they could hold the launch event in Third Space. He asked me about the café and the motivation behind it. I explained our vision of a business with the city's well-being at its heart. He was enthused. Where did the motivation for seeking the well-being of the city come from? I explained I was a follower of Jesus and that the notion of serving others because Jesus first served me was my motivation. His face grew serious and, for a moment, I thought the humanists would take their business elsewhere. Instead, he leaned back and looked up. When his gaze came down again, there was a smile on his face. "I like that," he said, "I like it."

Another way that Third Space expresses its social commitment is through a monthly event known as the Square Meal. On the last Friday of each month, all of the tables are pushed toward each other—everyone sits together. The menu is based on a simple theme; everyone eats the same food. A local project has five minutes to tell the story of what they are involved in doing and how others can help them. At the end of the evening, people are asked to put whatever they can afford into a box rather than pay a normal bill. The contents of that box go to the project that has been highlighted.

The Theology of Creating Space

I have studied theology, though I'm no professional theologian. But the depth and impact of what we saw in the first few months of Third Space forced me into "on the job" theological reflection on what was happening. The goal had been to develop a business that created and managed a space. But people were experiencing something more. Eventually, I went back to a passage in Miroslav Volf's *Exclusion and Embrace*. Written as a theological response to the Yugoslav Wars, the book explores the notion of creating space for the other, the outsider, the enemy. The gospel message, Volf says, is that God created space for us through the cross: "We, the others—we, the enemies—are embraced by the divine persons who love us with the same love with which they love each other and therefore make space for us within their own eternal embrace."

The idea of creating space in the city had been more theologically significant than we realised. When we set out to create space for "the others," for people of all kinds, that action was a reflection of what God has done for us. We shouldn't have been taken aback that people were moved. They may not have understood why this space was important, but they could feel it nonetheless.

Motivation and Motive

"Exactly what it says on the tin"

In the 1990s, Ronseal, a company that manufactures wood stain, started a famous advertising campaign for their quick-drying solution. "So," the ad went, "if you've got wood to stain and you want it to dry quickly, use Ronseal quick-drying woodstain. It does exactly what it says on the tin." That final phrase, "It does exactly what it says on the tin," became a part of common parlance to describe something that's straightforward with no hidden agenda.

As we launched Third Space, we wanted that to be true of us. We didn't want people to dig into our story and find that we were really a church or a charity masquerading as a business. So we had to be a business, not a charity, by employing the best candidates for jobs, welcoming all customers equally, and not seeking special favours from suppliers.

We kept the "good cause" flag stored away when we opened. This allowed people to come in and discover what Third Space was for themselves. One challenge was that some churchgoers came in expecting to be served by a fellow churchgoer, to find bookshelves lined only with religious literature, or to hear worship music playing on our sound system. Gradually, church folk got the message that Third Space was offering space to every tribe, not just their tribe. And, in time, several ended up using Third Space as a venue for evangelistic courses.

When customers learned that Third Space was a social business, people started asking questions. Some of our customers are lawyers, so the questioning was not superficial. Additionally, Google was forthcoming with details about my previous career. But by the time these questions arose, two things were clear to our regulars. We had not made a big deal about being a social business, and we had not tried to evangelize them while they were having their coffee. As they quizzed the staff, they discovered that many had no connection to church—we hadn't just hired from our own tribe. In the end, they seemed to love Third Space more, not less.

Over time, we learned to draw a distinction between motive and motivation when we answered people's questions. On the one hand, "Why are you doing this?" can mean, "Where did the motivation come from? What motivated you to start this?" On the other hand, "Why do it?" can mean, "What are you hoping to achieve through this? What is your motive?" To put it another way, motivation lies at the start of the process. Motive lies at the end.

Jesus draws a distinction between motivation and motive when he challenges the disciples in John 13:14-17: "Now that I, your Lord and Teacher, have washed your feet, you also should wash one another's feet. I have set you an example that you should do as I have done for you.... Now that you know these things, you will be blessed if you do them."

Jesus provides both motive and motivation. The motivation is, "Now that I, your Lord and teacher, have washed your feet..." When they wash people's feet in the future, someone may ask, "Why are you doing this?" and they will legitimately answer, "Jesus washed our feet and that motivates us to wash yours." But Jesus also provides them with a motive: "Now that you know these things, you will be blessed if you do them."

The distinction between motivation and motive helped clarify thinking around the "why" question for Third Space. We were clear that Third Space had a gospel-motivation, not an evangelism-motive.

A Cultural Legacy

A connection between religion and social benefit may not matter in other cultural contexts, but in Ireland, it matters a lot. Here we have a troubling legacy of evangelism linked to mercy ministry. For us, the Ronseal test mattered—were we doing what we said on the tin? Cultural and theological reflection are essential to find the right way of explaining your mission. In the heat of setting up a new business, it's easy to think that this "theoretical" thinking can be left for another day. But if it isn't done early when values and motives take root, the gaps will be exposed—the city tends to do that.

Social Business and Gospel Ecosystems in the City

As Third Space progressed, I also worked alongside church planters, mercy project leaders, and all kinds of "normal" people interested in growing a gospel movement in the city. We met together, ate together, and ran workshops and seminars. We received helpful input from Redeemer City to City, the London Institute for Contemporary Christianity, Perimeter Church in Atlanta, and 3DM Discipleship in England. Churches were planted and mercy projects initiated.

Working on these fronts and Third Space simultaneously often felt like having a split personality. I would meet church planters to encourage them in their church-planting and then head off to meet café owners or businesspeople to pick their brains about my social business idea. I saw puzzled expressions on church planters' faces as they tried to connect their vision for a church with my vision for a non-religious café. Business people were suspicious of the "religious do-gooder" wanting to start a business to change the city.

Discovering Connections

Study, thought, conversation, and incessant dreaming finally produced some clear thoughts for me. First, social business is a third way—neither a normal business nor a charity. Having been taught to think of the gospel as a third way, neither religion nor irreligion, that parallel seemed significant. The gospel dwells in the tension between law and licence: "What shall we say then? Shall we go on sinning so that grace may increase?" (Romans 6:1) It refuses to accept that there are only two options to obey God's laws or ignore them. The gospel offers a way to fulfill the law without slavish adherence to the letter.

So too should social businesses accept certain truths or rules about business, but subvert those rules by adopting a posture of grace or benevolence towards the city. Social business dwells in the tension between business and charity. It doesn't treat profit as a dirty word, but also refuses to accept that business is *only* about making a profit. It offers a way of working in business without being enslaved by it.

Second, Christians are called to serve the city and a social business is a tangible way to do it. Third Space was started from the conviction that if it ever got the chance to open its doors, it would be to the benefit of the surrounding area.

Third, this kind of initiative was never intended as an alternative to church planting or mercy projects. I had travelled enough with City to City to see that church planting is crucial for city transformation. Church plants in Dublin have reached people with the gospel in creative ways. As these Jesus-following communities grew in size, so too did their desire to see their city changed by the Jesus message. Alongside them, gospel-motivated mercy projects have alleviated pressing concerns such as unemployment and addiction.

The Third Space project was not intended to displace or replace any of this work. Rather, Third Space was intended as another dimension, another expression of a movement committed to sharing with others the work God has done in our own lives. Though evangelism was not our motive, we could still be an important part of a gospel movement. We would do good in the city, contributing to its well being. While Jesus followers believe that new churches are an enormous contribution to the city's wellbeing, many European citizens do not agree. A social business is a chance to do good in a way that is more socially acceptable and prompts an explanation.

Another advantage is that a well-planned, well-run social business will not create a financial drain on the movement because it will source its start-up funding outside of the usual sources and will generate its own finances in time. Some movements may even be tempted to use profits generated to fund gospel work, but wisdom may dictate otherwise. Remember the Ronseal ad: "exactly what it says on the tin."

Social businesses provide connection to a whole new set of people that might never go near a church, including staff, suppliers, other businesses, city officials, and local community groups. The nature of the work can mean that these relationships go deeper than simple transactions and lead to conversations about bigger issues.

The social capital of organised religion in Dublin is at a pretty low ebb right now. There have been too many scandals, too many power games, too many attempts to control people's behaviour. Many are loath to listen to the church simply because it's the church. But when the church is a businesswoman whose social enterprise has created measurable social benefits, then people listen—not because it's the church, but because it's good. Social businesses that work open doors.

Social businesses can engage in all kinds of activity—manufacturing, design, recycling, education. But a social business seeking to be part of a gospel movement should give attention to food and hospitality. It is significant that Jesus teaches his disciples to remember him with a meal. At meals, hosts create space at their table for others, those who don't own the table but get to sit there. What takes place around a table is more than the sum of its parts. If a social enterprise can run a business that creates space at the table for the outsider, then they mirror the work of God in a special way.

Step Out Onto the Road

It takes more space than this paper affords to lay out a plan for social enterprises as an intrinsic part of a gospel movement alongside church planting, mercy ministries, and faith in work initiatives, but a few simple steps might start the journey.

List the five most important social problems facing your city.

As you walk your city and pray for it, what social problems stand out? How long have the problems been there? How pervasive are they? What solutions have been attempted?

Do some theological analysis of the problems.

All of our problems have roots in rebellion against God, but dig deeper. Does the Bible give insight into the reason and possible solutions? Do the teachings and examples of Jesus provide insight and help? As you do this work, watch out for the problem that stands out and demands your attention.

Talk to the people already working on this problem.

Don't think that no one else has seen or worked on this problem. In every city, there are people who care for their city and want to solve its problems. Most of these people won't share your faith or convictions. But they will still have stories worth listening to and learning from.

Talk to the business people in your church and your city.

Tell them about the concept of a social business and paint the picture of starting a business to solve a social problem. Talk to people in the business sector you want to join. If the problem is money lenders exploiting the poor, talk to bankers and other financiers. If the problem is housing, talk to builders and planners. Maintain the posture of learning.

Find Jesus-following entrepreneurs.

Dealing with the problem will require people who know how to start things. An entrepreneur is someone who sees a problem as an opportunity—their eyes light up when someone tells them something can't be done because it sounds like an invitation. Find Jesus-following entrepreneurs and challenge them to start social businesses to solve your city's intractable problems.

Do some dreaming.

The question that led to the beginning of Third Space was this: "Séan, if you could do anything you wanted in life and there were no restrictions, what would you do?" Ask yourself those kinds of questions.

Start writing a plan.

There are 33 versions of the Third Space start up plan, but without Version 1, it never would have happened. After all the talking, listening, praying, exploring, and dreaming, someone needs to write down some possible next steps. That's how businesses start—even social ones.

And Finally...

Social businesses on their own, even when led by Jesus-following business geniuses, will not transform a city. But my contention is that they should have a place in a healthy gospel-ecosystem alongside church plants, charities serving needs, creative initiatives, and workplace training. The particular strength of the social business model in such a system is that it provides a visible demonstration of a third option that is neither business nor charity, even before they learn that the gospel is an invitation to a third way of living with God.

Chapter 5

Transforming the Gap

The Arts as Mediator Between the Church and the City

SUDE HOPE

Introduction

To be able to transform a gap, you have to leave familiar ground and alight to a new level.

There is a gap between the church and the city. The gap is a space.

The space is not empty. It is full of opportunity.

There is space between the church and the city. Shared space. Mysterious space.

Spaces between are full of possibilities, orphaned realms waiting to be embraced, wildwater basins carrying the cries of our cities, platforms hungry to be brought to life.

These spaces exist between you and me, between our outer and inner worlds, between the visible world and God's mysteries, between alien and familiar, between here and there.

Abundant spaces are waiting to be cultivated as creative playfields of life and its Inventor. Art promotes "cross"-cultural encounter in these spaces and enable new forms of dialogue. They create an alternate realm that allows shared processes of both like-minded and diverse people. Collaboration, dialogue, and a common search are the keys to foster community in these spaces. Art brings about all three of them.

Churches are called to transform in-between spaces into vibrant, life-affirming meeting places by encouraging dialogue and embracing various groups in their cities. They are called to foster encounters and facilitate renewal and creativity. Art is highly effective for accomplishing this calling. It submits a new kind of encounter and fosters movement.

Space

The Space Between

A space between church and city can be seen as a space of division or a meeting place, depending on our perspective. The way we talk about it is important. Churches are often considered strangers in our European secular contexts. In return, churches often consider phenomena of society as bizarre. And so the space between is often considered a "gap," a term that focuses on differences instead of commonalities.

Churches tend to expect people from the city to come into a church and adapt to its culture. To fit in, the city has to conform to the rules and expectations of the church. Tim Chester writes in *Gospel-Centred Church*, "Church is where we feel safe and comfortable. Church is where non-Christians feel embarrassed and awkward. We offer people the gospel, but on our terms and territory."[24]

Yes, there are differences between the city and the church., but wherever there are differences, there are similarities, too. Imagine if a church had such a positive regard for its surrounding culture that it focused on the commonalities between city and church and transformed the gap into a space for discovery. Imagine the gap transformed by fearless openness and acceptance. Are we not called to welcome the alien and the "other" on the grounds of God's unconditional love?

Imagine the gap transformed into a space where strangers become friends. A space that welcomes round and edgy people and embraces odd fishes, weirdos, and well-educated know-it-alls. Imagine a space of renewal, a space where people search together, a space for dialogue, a space to find and be found.

The space between the city and the church is only a gap if we allow it to be. If we are willing, we can transform the gap into a space where transformation happens. Yes, it's unsafe and challenging. But it's worth it.

Stepping into the space between takes courage. It means leaving well-known territory, convenient habits, safety, knowledge, and more behind to explore a new field shared with others.

It requires a step toward encounter, a step toward a common here-and-now shared with strangers. It's a step into God's favorite playfield.

There are many spaces in-between that are potential meeting places. One of them with the power to transform is art.

Third Space 2 Go

> "A place that is a leveler is, by its nature, an inclusive place."[25] – R. Oldenburg

The idea of third spaces as neutral areas to connect communities was introduced by urban sociologist Ray Oldenburg in his book *The Great Good Place*. Third spaces are spaces that are not work, not church, and not home. They offer safety, freedom, possibilities for shared conversation, and easy access. In church contexts, they allow members to investigate urban contexts and to meet people halfway.[26] A café, for example, provides delicious common ground.[27]

Art itself functions as third space, but of a different sort. Unlike a café, art is detached from a physical location. This creates challenges, but also opportunities. With its non-physical attributes, art opens further possibilities in encounter and endows dialogue of a different quality.

Art lives between church and the city—it mediates between them. Art is common ground where equal participation and shared experiences are possible.

Art also dwells between God and us.

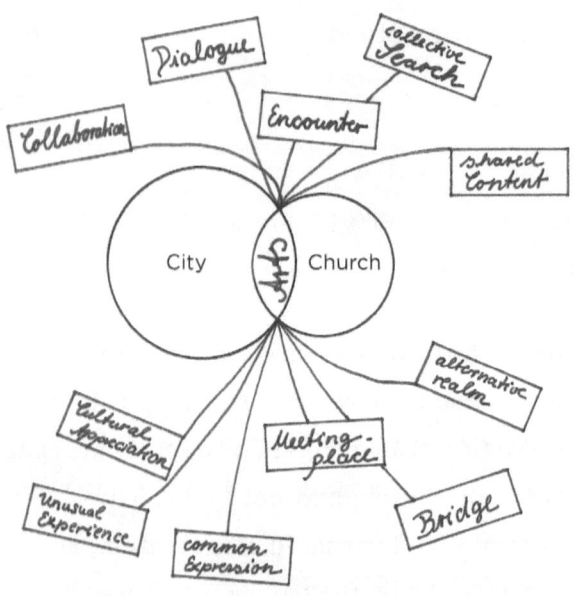

The arts as in-between space.

The core of art unfolds in between—between what's there and what will be, between letting go and finding, between perceiving and acting, between natural and invisible, between reality and fantasy, between I and thou, between God and humans, between outer and inner world, between here and there, between giver and receiver. It creates an alternative realm. It is a third space.

This realm acts as an alternative medium and provides a platform for a dialogue of different quality. It allows exchange and inspiration that reaches beyond cognitive layers.

If art is part of shared creative processes, it adds manifold opportunities to foster communities and relationships. If you've ever participated in a creative project that engaged your community, such as performing a musical or building a playground in your neighborhood, you may have experienced the social impact and connective power of creating together.

Art gives room for shared experiences: it bunches interests, creates a common focus and subject matter, channels attention, and turns people into allies. It encourages openness, creates cross-connections, and gives opportunity for common expression. It is also an opportunity for the church to express appreciation for the city's culture and a chance to really see the city and its topics, atmospheres, and heart motions.

Art is needed as an alternative and stirring realm for those who usually wouldn't connect to see each other, to meet each other, to touch each other and to be touched by God—to relate with each others' stories and shared experiences.

In the following pages, we will focus on characteristics of art and artistic processes that help to strengthen the relationship between church and city and transform gaps into spaces of change.

Core and Necessity

Words & Figments

Words are at the very core of creation.

> *In the beginning was the Word, and the Word was with God, and the Word was God. He was with God in the beginning. Through him all things were made; without him nothing was made that has been made.* —John 1:1-3

Everything that came into existence came through spoken word. God calls himself Word. Speaking is creating. Sound and sense breathed form and being into existence.

Observing God as Creator, we see an inconceivable, incredible, inexhaustible, detail-loving, fanciful, overflowing, devoted, extravagant, and incomprehensible sculptor who causes the depths of our being to stir and showcases himself endlessly through his oeuvre.

All of our senses are invited to discover divine mysteries through aesthetic ways. They are designed as an invitation to embrace truth and to descry God's character expressed through aesthetics, pointing us toward love and appreciation.

Created in his image, we are called to collaborate in creative action. In creating, we experience our *homoiousia*, our

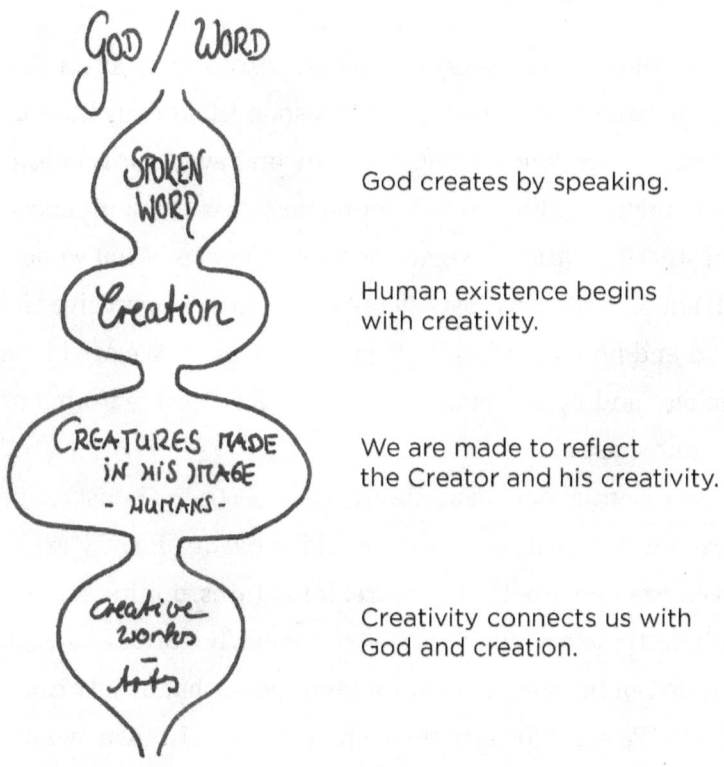

God creates by speaking.

Human existence begins with creativity.

We are made to reflect the Creator and his creativity.

Creativity connects us with God and creation.

The origin of arts.

similarity with our creator. We have been created to create, made to draw on creation, and called to correspond with creatures. There is an abundance for us to explore and infinite ways waiting for us to express heavenly stories. Let's collaborate creatively with our maker.

Aesthetics & Beauty

Aesthetics are always present. Aesthetics affect us. Whether we value them or not, we respond. Our daily life, our choices, atmospheres, things we own, and even our relationships—including the one with our own selves—are influenced by aesthetics. We are designed as sensual beings. What we see, feel, smell, hear, and taste determines how we perceive the world and how we relate to things and beings. We are being touched, and at the same time, we touch our environment with our senses.

An essential field in aesthetics that has been almost rationalized in the postmodern art world is beauty. Beauty exists as a consequence of God's nature. It nurtures, uplifts, and upholds us. It fosters affection. Dietrich von Hildebrand states in Volume I of his last publication, *Aesthetics*, that beauty causes love. We sense beauty through aesthetics. In turn, beauty is made to lead us to love. There is a reciprocity between love and beauty.

If one finds aesthetic value in something or someone, he relates to it in a positive way and develops some kind of love. In turn, if someone loves something or someone, he perceives a broader realm of beauty attached to the person or thing.[28]

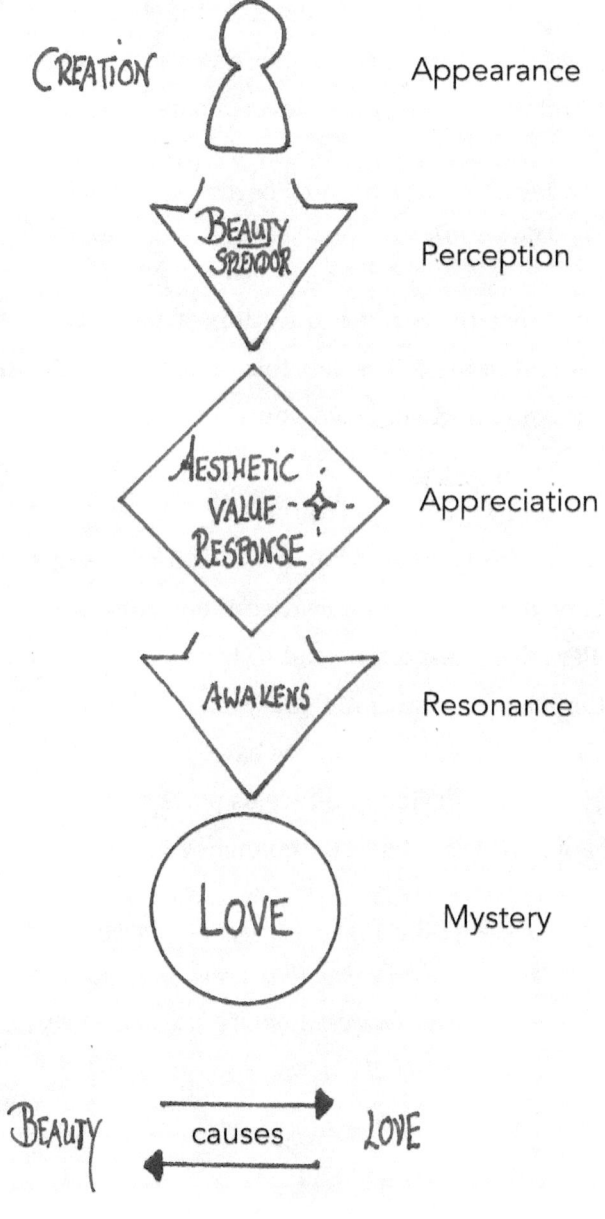

The relation of beauty and love.

The more beauty we perceive, the greater our love. The more we love, the more we perceive as beautiful. Both bring about relation and a deeper level of connection.

> *Beauty is not in the eye of the beholder. Instead, we agree on what is beautiful.* —Stefan Sagmeister[29]

True beauty is not a question of taste, but attached to things and beings. It is sensible without specific knowledge or certain expertise. Have you ever heard someone say the sunset looked ugly? Every human has a predisposed sense of beauty, and we agree on true beauty.

True beauty is essential. It is food for our souls, it points to God and helps us to relate with our environment.

Perceived aesthetics lead to revelation. Appreciated aesthetics lead to adoration. Beauty leads to love.

Sensing a realm of beauty exceeding natural appearance connects us with God and reveals parts of his nature. In turn, sight of his divine character changes us.

> *And we all, who with unveiled faces contemplate the Lord's glory, are being transformed into his image with ever-increasing glory, which comes from the Lord, who is the Spirit.* —2 Corinthians 3:18

God changes us through sight. Sight of himself—the ultimate source of beauty transforms us into his image. We are inclined to be changed by contemplation and perception. What we see changes our appearance and action.

Beauty and aesthetics provoke change in our relation with our context as well. They are necessary for our church communities in building relation with our cities and shaping society through revealing the beauty of our Creator..

Effect—Art as Mediator

Now that we have considered the value and place of art in the church, how does it affect the church's relationship with the city? Art helps church plants accomplish important aims: Connection, Contextualization, and Transformation.

Connection

Art touches and connects. Art touches in unusual ways and reaches us in places that are far beyond understanding. If art speaks, it communicates in a quality that differs from everyday communication such as news, emails, messages, and commercials. There is a special quality in autotelic artworks.

When artworks speak, they often touch something in us that resists being reduced to words. Touch is always mutual. Every time we are touched, we touch at the same time. If we create or contemplate art, it is always a mutual process. It is a dialogical process that takes place between the piece and the recipient or creator.

> *I touch and I am being touched. What we call the self appears to us in contact. When we shake hands, we touch each other. A relationship starts with sensory perception, so a handshake creates a relationship-endowing moment.* — *Peter Sinapius* [30]

Even a handshake is a short moment of mutual touch. Being touched is always intimate. If we are touched by an art piece—emotionally, spiritually—we also experience intimacy. If we share this experience with another person, it additionally connects us with each other. Touch endows relationships. Shared experiences of touch connect. Take the delightful experience of a deeply stirring concert, for example, or a walk veiled in the beauty of a breathtaking piece of architecture. After your experience together, you will feel more connected. In the same way, art enriches community through touch and connectivity with God, the works, and each other.

To be able to enter an artistic process or to perceive an art piece attentively, it is necessary to be open and to put judgmentalism aside. Each piece of art has its own agenda.[31] To experience it, we have to be curious, explore, discover, question, search, and find.

These traits allow us to connect not just with diverse art, but diverse people, too. We are able to perceive others in a different way when we put our knowledge aside and open up to new experiences. Art endows openness, which can create a relationship between church and city.

Art is connective. Art enables us to transform cold places into meeting places through touch, atmosphere, dialogue, and experience. Art can abide boundaries and turn gaps into spaces for encounter. True art is highly connective at its core. It connects people with each other and, at its best, individuals with the ultimate source of creativity and mysteries behind the works. Its connectivity has several directions—intrinsic, inward, outward, horizontal, vertical, diagonal, circular, concentric.

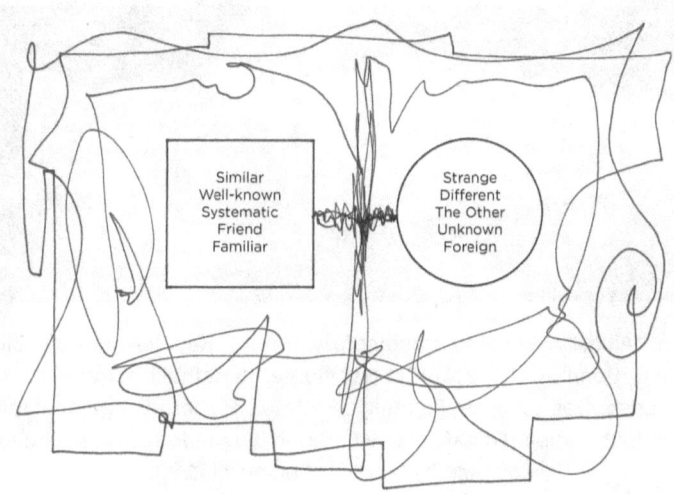

Similar and other.

Art derives from relation. In its original form, it springs out of search, out of movement, out of seeking the true, good, and beautiful. True art reveals, touches, reaches out, enlightens, seeks to speak, and to be a counterpart—of you, of me, of us.

> *This is the eternal origin of art: that a human being is confronted by a form that wants to become a work through him.* —Martin Buber[32]

Title: "All art has been contemporary." Photo: Kay Riechers. VG Bild-Kunst, Bonn 2010. Artworks: Hamburger Kunsthalle. Caspar David Friedrich. Das Eismeer, Painting 1823/24. Richard Long. Mountain Circle, Installation. Frankfurt 1991. Sammlung Lafrenz. Original quote: Neon sign by Maurizio Nannucci, 1999.

Contextualization

Art is always a room and a medium of reflection for its time and context.

Observing art and diving into your city's cultural scene will tell you most of its present topics, attitudes, dispositions, values, concerns, desires, and dreams. Art reveals the soul of society. Creating art in turn requires an ability to perceive the world around and to capture and process its material. It necessitates skills to step into dialogue with the artistic material and the human audience behind it.

Both skills are beneficial in church planting. They will help us get a deeper understanding of our context and a greater sensitivity for the people we share life with in our city. We don't need to be artists to do so. Time to explore our city's cultural scene and space to engage creativity and creatives will make the greatest difference.

Perceiving the world we are in happens when we break our routine and pay attention with all of our senses. Hearing, listening, tasting, feeling, and smelling our context will help us build relation in "sense-ible" ways. Senses make sense, and, if they are used naturally, they enable insights, "outsights" and conversations that lead to sense and truth.

Transformation

Creating a piece of art and planting a church have a lot in common.

> *A creative act requires two things: You have to shape things and you have to allow things. —M. Schleske[33]*

Abilities necessary for creating art can be helpful in church planting. The outcomes from an artistic process promote transformation.

If I am creating a painting, I am always stepping into a dialogue with the piece that evolves; I am creating through a transformational process. It is a process of observing, searching, shaping, forming, resonating, and finding. Layer after layer of paint is added in different textures, different formations with breaks in action, in between where I observe what has occurred on the canvas and listen to what the piece demands. It is a dialogic process—a process of call and response and a process of change.

In the same way, a church planter acts like a sculptor or painter forming the body of the church in collaboration with God, listening, acting, moulding, composing, resonating, and shaping what has been placed before him. It is a process of call and response and a creative act to plant and form the church.

Engaging the arts will provoke implicit learning, promote creative skills, and extend social abilities. Aesthetic competencies such as being present and open, having awareness, using lateral thinking, and leaning into creativity enable you to foster community and transformation in quickly changing times.[34] Embracing creative methods and artistic elements will help you to refresh your church community and to build relationships with your city in a powerful way.

Three Practical Examples of Artistic Interventions In-between

Following are three brief examples of artistic interventions in different cultural contexts. They were designed to create space for "cross"-cultural encounter and to foster community.

Culture Dine / Germany.

Culture Dine, Hamburg

Culture Dine is an open, pop-up dinner with small cultural "bites." Each "happening" provides opportunities to share food and short bites—contributions from different media such as music, poetry, pictures, paintings, and short films on a given topic.[35] The shared material can be your own creation or from other sources. This means everyone is able to participate, whether they are artistically inclined or not. Every evening offers time to share food at one long table, time to share contributions, and three segments of creative action where participants are guided in an artistic process. Interactive elements encourage dialogue and impulses inspire creative action. At the end of every evening, a piece of "community art" is created with the materials created throughout the evening.

During one happening, for example, the topic was "Beginning and End." Throughout the evening, participants drew on the table, made little sculptures, and completed free-writing compositions. String that had been placed at the table functioned as material for interactive sequences and became an installation to direct which table-fellows added their pieces to the group's structure. The collective works—in this case, a community text composed of freewriting sentences and an installation—were made of diverse material ranging from sad to funny, from concrete to abstract parts.

Many Culture Dine participants mentioned that they have been inspired and touched by the variety of perspectives, the atmosphere of the evenings, and the opportunity to meet people outside of their usual routine.

A basic rule in this project is to use well-known spaces that are part of the city's cultural scene and are outside a physical church building. Easy-access and low-level locations with big windows help people to stumble in spontaneously and add to a more diverse mix of people.

Space2Create—After-Work Chillout and Paint, Tel Aviv

Space2Create: After Work Chillout & Paint was one of three formats designed and implemented for a young church plant in Tel Aviv's vibrant neighborhood of Florentin. The format was simple, but favored by Tel Aviv's artsy inhabitants. Each evening offered a time of tasty chill-out and loose warm-up before a guided artistic process took place. During one evening, for example, the group experimented with different printing techniques. They created individual as well as community works on a six-meter-long sheet, sharing discoveries they made during the process with each other. The focus in this project was on arts and creative action, which allowed participants with very different positions to work together and step into a dialogue. Most participants didn't come from church backgrounds and hadn't been to the space before.

Space 2 Create / Israel.

Out of this project, new connections arose. The space became better known, and new initiatives emerged. An urban gardening project was born out of it and some relationships are still thriving.

Art Workshops and Interactive Eatart Experience, Czech Republic

During a Music & Arts Festival initiated by a group of believers from different churches in the Czech countryside, an artist-in-residence created an interactive Eatart experience. A diverse crowd of people attended and explored the topic of "differences in creative ways."

Eat+Art Experience / Czech Republic.

At a long table surrounded by a cooking station, an interactive installation, and nature, participants were guided in a creative process with writing, drawing, cooking, and more. During a diversity meal, they shared inspiration, artworks, and food. A young scientist who participated mentioned two days later that she had been deeply touched by the encounters she experienced during the workshops and that she had never undergone something like Eatart. She was worn out by her city life but felt comforted and encouraged through the experience. Two days later, she joined a church service and began to read the Bible.

Conclusion: God's Campsite

For there is one God and one mediator between God and mankind, the man Christ Jesus. —1 Timothy 2:5

There is a mediator in between, a grandmaster of encounter, a lover of all souls, a versed artist of a welcoming culture, and a dissident in our meritocracy. Created skillfully in his image, we are master students of his arts and called to mediate in similar manners with radiant creativity.

Engaging the arts will enable us to fashion transformation in fast-changing times and to step into relevant and compelling dialogue that leaves a mark on the cities we live in. Art is an invitation for us and others to share common ground. It is an opportunity to leave well-known territory behind and step into wildwaters of change in an alternative space. It allows us to be present, open, and connective. It is an invitation to create and to find, to let go, and to sense what makes sense. Art is a change maker, an incubator for innovation, and a meeting place for everyone.

Art as a space between allows a deeper relation with our cities. It enables us to overcome boundaries and to collaborate with familiars and strangers to sculpt society:

> *Created creative in the image of the creator*
> *Designed with senses making sense*

Kissed by grace
Called to embrace
Same but different
Made to make a difference
Sent to go with wings to flow
Alive to share life
Twinkling to revive
Out of the dust
onto this worlds map
Called to take a step
Empowered to transform the gap. —Sude Hope

God dwells in the in-between. Let's engage in art and sit down to marvel. He is already waiting on the threshold.

Notes

1. J. H. Bavinck, *The Church between Temple and Mosque* (Grand Rapids: Eerdmans, 1966), 38.

2. Stefan Paas, "Religious Consciousness in a Post-Christian Culture" (Journal of Reformed Theology, 2012), 35-55.

3. See Miroslav Volf, *A Public Faith* (Grand Rapids: Brazos Press, 2011); Os Guinness, *Renaissance: The Power of the Gospel However Dark the Times* (Downers Grove: IVP Books, 2014); and Jonathan Sacks, "On Creative Minorities: The 2013 Erasmus Lecture," *First Things*, January 2014.

4. Andy Crouch, *Culture Making: Rediscovering our Creative Calling* (Downers Grove: IVP Books, 2013).

5. Bobette Buster, as quoted in Jon Tyson, Jon and Heather Grizzle, *A Creative Minority: Influencing Culture through Redemptive Participation*. 2016, 26.

6. Miroslav Volf, *A Public Faith*, 7.

7. Makoto Fujimura, *Culture Care: Reconnecting with Beauty for our Common Life* (Downers Grove: IVP Books, 2017), 40.

8. Jonathan Sacks, "On Creative Minorities."

9. Timothy Keller, *Center Church* (Grand Rapids: Zondervan, 2012), 333.

10. Fujimura, 59.

11. Alan Jacobs, "The Watchmen: What Became of the Christian Intellectuals?" *Harper's*. September 2016 issue. https://harpers.org/archive/2016/09/the-watchmen/?single=1.

12. William Wilberforce, as quoted in Os Guinness, *Renaissance*, 29.

13. "After this I looked, and behold, a great multitude that no one could number, from every nation, from all tribes and peoples and languages, standing before the throne and before the Lamb, clothed in white robes, with palm branches in their hands."

14. For more information, visit http://icpnetwork.nl/?la=en.

15. Disclaimer: Of course, society also needs network churches—churches in which people of similar societal backgrounds meet and connect with each other. In these churches, people can learn a lot from each other, too. However, in my opinion, the best way to meet the biblical ideal of various people and cultures worshiping together is a church in which people from different ages, social classes, and ethnicities blend together.

16. John Piper, *Let the Nations Be Glad: The Supremacy of God in Missions* (Baker Book House, 1993).

17. The prognosis for the Netherlands is that the number of citizens from different cultural backgrounds will grow from three to six million, within a total of eighteen million inhabitants (https://www.cbs.nl/nl-nl/nieuws/2017/51/prognose-18-4-miljoen-inwoners-in-2060).

18. In her book *Foreign to Familiar*, Sarah Lanier makes helpful distinctions between "hot-climate" and "cold-climate" cultures. We ask all our church members to read this book to get an easy understanding of cultural diversity within our congregation.

19. Stefan Paas, *Church Planting in the Secular West* (Grand Rapids, W.B. Eerdmans Publishing Company), 94.

20. David Bosch, *Transforming Mission: Paradigm Shifts in Theology of Mission* (Maryknoll, Orbis Books, 1991), 332.

21. Church planter Rob Krause explains that the churches in Italy don't talk about a "refugee crisis," https://www.thegospelcoalition.org/article/church-italy-doesnt-see-migrants-crisis/

22. Moses Alagbe, *The Church is Boring!: If It is Not Relevant* (Galilee Media), 47.

23. Dietrich Bonhoeffer, *Life Together* (HarperCollins Publishers).

24. Tim Chester. *Gospel-Centred Church* (UK: The Good Book Company, 2002), 25

25. Ray Oldenburg. *The Great Good Place: Cafés, Coffee Shops, Bookstores, Bars, Hair Salons, and Other Hangouts at the Heart of a Community.* (New York: Marlow & Company, 1999), 24.

26. Nathan Hill, *Why I Love the Third Space.* http://dmergent.org/articles/2012/04/10/why-i-love-the-third-space.

27. Matt Busby, *Three Practices for Third Space Churches.* https://www.christianitytoday.com/edstetzer/2016/september/three-practices-for-third-space-churches.html.

28. Dietrich von Hildebrand, *Aesthetics: Volume I* (Ohio: Dietrich von Hildebrand Legacy Project, 2016) XXIX, 451.

29. Stefan Sagmeister (presentation, Schön Conference, Augsburg, June 16, 2018).

30. Peter Sinapius, *"Wie ist es, eine Farbe zu sein?": Über Kunst und Liebe, das Schweigen und die Gegenwart.* (Berlin: Frank & Timme, 2013), 15-16.

31. Hans-Georg Gadamer, *Die Aktualität des Schönen* (Stuttgart: Philipp Reclam jun. GmbH & Co., 1977).

32. Martin Buber, *Ich und Du* (Heidelberg: Verlag Lambert Schneider, 1983), 60.

33. Martin Schleske, *Der Klang: Vom unerhörten Sinn des Lebens* (München: Koesel Verlag, 2010), 99.

34. Hannes Jahn and Peter Sinapius, *Transformation: Künstlerische Arbeit in Veränderungsprozessen. Grundlagen und Konzepte: Band 1.* (Hamburg: HPB University Press, 2015), 16.

35. I use this term instead of "event" to emphasize their artistic approach. From my perspective, "happening" is more suitable because such evenings are designed as artwork—they are framed and enacted as living pieces of art or social sculptures.

Bibliography

Chapter 2

Crouch, Andy. *Culture Making: Rediscovering our Creative Calling*. Downers Grove: IVP Books, 2013.

Fujimura, Makoto. *Culture Care: Reconnecting with Beauty for our Common Life*. Downers Grove: IVP Books, 2017.

Guder, Darrell, ed. *Missional Church: A Vision for the Sending of the Church in North America*. Grand Rapids: Eerdmans, 1998.

Guinness, Os. *Renaissance: The Power of the Gospel However Dark the Times*. Downers Grove: IVP Books, 2014.

Hunter, James Davidson. *To Change the World: The Irony, Tragedy, and Possibility of Christianity in the Late Modern World*. New York and Oxford: Oxford University Press, 2010.

Jacobs, Alan. "The Watchmen: What Became of the Christian Intellectuals?" *Harper's*. September 2016 issue. https://harpers.org/archive/2016/09/the-watchmen/?single=1.

Keller, Timothy. *Center Church: Doing Balanced, Gospel-Centered Ministry in Your City*. Grand Rapids: Zondervan, 2012.

Kierkegaard, Søren. *The Essential Kierkegaard*, eds. Howard V. Hong and Edna H. Hong. Princeton: Princeton University Press, 2000.

Larsen, Josh. *Movies Are Prayers: How Films Voice our Deepest Longings*. Downers Grove: IVP Books, 2017.

McManus, Erwin Raphael. *The Artisan Soul: Crafting Your Life into a Work of Art*. New York: HarperOne, 2014.

Newbigin, Lesslie. *The Gospel in a Pluralist Society*. Grand Rapids: Eerdmans, 1989.

Sacks, Jonathan. "On Creative Minorities: The 2013 Erasmus Lecture." *First Things*. January 2014. https://www.firstthings.com/article/2014/01/on-creative-minorities.

Taylor, Charles. *A Secular Age*. Cambridge, MA: The Belknap Press of Harvard University Press, 2007.

Tyson, Jon, and Heather Grizzle. *A Creative Minority: Influencing Culture through Redemptive Participation*. 2016.

Volf, Miroslav. *A Public Faith*. Grand Rapids: Brazos Press, 2011.

Wright, N. T. *The New Testament and the People of God*. Minneapolis: Fortress Press, 1992.

Chapter 3

Alagbe, Moses. *The Church is Boring!: If It is Not Relevant*. Galilee Media, 2015.

Bonhoeffer, Dietrich. *Life Together: The Classic Exploration of Christian Community*. HarperCollins, 1954.

Bosch, David. *Transforming Mission: Paradigm Shifts in Theology of Mission*. Maryknoll, Orbis Books, 1991.

Lanier, Sarah A. *Foreign to Familiar: A Guide to Understanding Hot- and Cold-Climate Cultures*. Hagerstown, McDougal Publishing, 2000.

Paas, Stefan. *Church Planting in the Secular West: Learning from the European Experience*. Grand Rapids, William B. Eerdmans Publishing Company, 2016.

Piper, John. *Let the Nations Be Glad: The Supremacy of God in Missions*. Baker Book House, 1993.

Paas, Stefan. *Vreemdelingen en Priesters: Christelijke Missie in een Postchristelijke Omgeving*. Zoetermeer, Uitgeverij Boekencentrum, 2015.

Further Reading

Bird, Matt. *Transformation: What is God Doing and How Do We Join In?* Leicestershire: Matador, 2017.

Breen, Mike. *Building a Discipling Culture: How to Release a Missional Movement by Discipling People Like Jesus Did.* Ministries International, 2013.

DeYoung, Kevin, and Greg Gilbert. *What is the Mission of the Church?: Making Sense of Social Justice, Shalom, and the Great Commission.* Wheaton: Crossway, 2011.

Keller, Timothy. *Generous Justice: How God's Grace Makes Us Just.* New York: Dutton, 2010.

Keller, Timothy. *Ministries of Mercy: The Call of the Jericho Road.* New Jersey: P&R Publishing, 2015.

Rainer, Thom, and Eric Geiger. *Simple Church: Returning to God's Process for Making Disciples.* Nashville: B&H Publishing Group, 2011.

Reitsma, Bernhard. *Kwetsbare Liefde: De Kerk, de Islam, en de Drie-Enige God.* Zoetermeer: Boekencentrum, 2017.

Stoorvogel, Henk. *Viva de Kerk!: 10 Principes voor de Kerk van Nu.* Utrecht: Kok, 2017.

Chapter 5

Bohnenkamp, Anne. *Es geht um Poesie.* Frankfurt am Main: S. Fischer Verlag GmbH, 2013.

Brandstätter, Ursula. *Erkenntnis durch Kunst: Theorie und Praxis der ästhetischen Transformation.* Wien, Köln, Weimar: Böhlau Verlag GmbH & Cie., 2013.

Buber, Martin. *Ich und Du: 11. Auflage.* Heidelberg: Verlag Lambert Schneider, 1983.

Busby, Matt. "Three Practices for Third Space Churches." https://www.christianitytoday.com/edstetzer/2016/september/three-practices-for-third-space-churches.html.

Dey, Sarita. "Essthetik: Philosophische & theoretische Annäherung an den Begriff 'Essthetik' als Ausdruck eines künstlerisch-kulinarischen Ansatzes zur Gemeinschaftsförderung." Bachelor's thesis, MSH Medical School, 2016.

Gadamer, Hans-Georg. *Die Aktualität des Schönen.* Stuttgart: Philipp Reclam jun. GmbH & Co., 1977.

Hill, Nathan. "Why I love the Third Space." http://dmergent.org/articles/2012/04/10/why-i-love-the-third-space.

Jahn, Hannes & Peter Sinapius. *Transformation: Künstlerische Arbeit in Veränderungsprozessen.Grundlagen und Konzepte: Band 1.* Hamburg: HPB University Press, 2015.

Oldenburg, Ray. *The Great Good Place: Cafés, Coffee Shops, Bookstores, Bars, Hair Salons, and Other Hangouts at the Heart of a Community.* New York: Marlowe & Company, 1999.

Sagmeisters, Stefan. Presentation at the Schön Conference, Augsburg, June 2018.

Schleske, Martin. *Der Klang: Vom unerhörten Sinn des Lebens.* München: Koesel Verlag, 2010.

Sinapius, Peter. "Wie ist es, eine Farbe zu sein?": Über Kunst und Liebe, das Schweigen und die Gegenwart. Berlin: Frank & Timme, 2013.

Timmis, Steve & Tim Chester. *Gospel Centred Church: Becoming the Community God Wants You to Be.* UK: The Good Book Company, 2009.

Von Hildebrand, Dietrich. *Aesthetics: Volume I.* Ohio: Dietrich von Hildebrand Legacy Project, 2016.

Wolf, Barbara. "Gegenwartskunst begegnet Expressive Arts: Zwei Kunstbegriffe im Vergleich." Master's thesis, MSH Medical School, 2011.

About the Authors

1 — How the Gospel Makes Us More Creative

Stephan Pues is the director of City to City Europe, which aims to create gospel movements throughout the cities of Europe. Originally from Bonn, he has served as the planter and pastor of Nordstern Church and a leader of the CTC D-A-CH network in Frankfurt. Stephan is married to Verena, and they have three children.

2 — At the Intersection of Faith and Culture

René Breuel is the Lead Pastor of Hopera, a church in central Rome that hopes to spark a movement of new churches in Italy, and is the author of The Paradox of Happiness. René loves his wife, Sarah, their two boys, and lemon and hazelnut gelato.

3 — Integral Life

Jurjen ten Brinke planted a multi-ethnic church called Hope for the North in Amsterdam in 2006. The church includes Persian, Kurdish, Pakistani, and Surinamese house churches. Previously, he worked among asylum seekers in the Netherlands. Jurjen is married to Marijke and they have three daughters and a son.

4 — Developing a Gospel-Shaped Coaching Business in the City

Seán Mullan is the founder and director of Third Space, a social business that runs a café and gathering space in the centre of Dublin. Seán previously worked in the merchant navy and as a church planter and pastor in Cork and Dublin. He is actively involved with City to City Europe and a Dublin Church Planting Network. Married to Ana for 34 years, they have three adult children and two wonderful grandchildren.

5 — Transforming the Gap

Sude Hope is a visual artist and community builder based in Germany. She studied Interior Design and Arts in Social Transformation and works with arts in mission and social change. Sude has designed and realized several community building and art projects in Europe, Asia, and Africa, and has connected churches and cities in creative ways.

www.ingramcontent.com/pod-product-compliance
Lightning Source LLC
Chambersburg PA
CBHW021955290426
44108CB00012B/1085